Love Songs

P9-DBJ-996

Wisdom from
Saint Bernard of Clairvaux

Jeanne Kun, Editor

theWORD
among us

The Word Among Us Press
9639 Doctor Perry Road
Ijamsville, Maryland 21754
ISBN: 0-932085-47-4

www.wau.org

Wisdom Series Editor: Patricia Mitchell
Cover design by David Crosson

Made and printed in the United States of America

Library of Congress Cataloging-in-Publication Data

Bernard, of Clairvaux, Saint, 1090 or 91-1153
    [Selections. English. 2001]
    Love songs: wisdom from Saint Bernard of Clairvaux / Jeanne Kun,
editor.
      p. cm.
    Includes bibliographical references.
    ISBN 0-932085-47-4
    1. Spiritual life-Catholic Church. I. Kun, Jeanne, 1951- II. Title.

BX2350.3 .B4713 2001
248.4'82—dc21

Table of Contents

Introduction

On that spring day in 1113 when young Bernard of Fontaines passed through the gates of one of the poorest and strictest monasteries in France, he was seeking a life of obscurity. There, tucked away from the eyes and concerns of the world, he yearned for a deeper union with the God whom he loved. Little did Bernard realize that he had actually stepped through the gateway leading to a celebrated public life. This monk from Burgundy would soon be recognized as the most eloquent and influential man of his age, a renowned voice heard all over Europe, a man who "carried the twelfth century on his shoulders."

Monk and mystic, theologian and preacher, diplomat and counselor, Bernard dominated his times by his extraordinary gifts and charismatic personality. The man who entered Cîteaux to seek God and live a hidden life ended up spending about one-third of his years as a monk away from his monastery. He crisscrossed Western Europe at the request of popes and kings, settled religious and political disputes, and advised churchmen and statesmen alike.

Yet it is Bernard, the lover of Christ, who shines through every other role he was called upon to play. His ever-deepening encounter with Jesus motivated and equipped him to take up an active and public life. Compelled by his zeal for God, Bernard willingly spent himself to defend and serve the church of God, the people of God, and the business of God in the society around him. But even as Bernard traveled across the continent, his heart always longed to return to his home among his fellow monks. More than anything, he treasured his times of intimacy with the Lord, when he could allow the love of his Savior to flood his heart and mind. And throughout these years, insights and thoughts from Bernard's agile mind and the meditations of his heart overflowed into his sermons and writings.

Bernard's written works are as extensive and varied as the many roles he played. And it is love—God's for Bernard and Bernard's for God—that permeates everything he wrote. The selections in this book, *Love Songs: Wisdom from Saint Bernard of Clairvaux,* are chosen from the vast collections of these writings, which include sermons, letters, essays, and treatises. Nearly nine hundred years after his death, Bernard's words are still full of a vitality and spiritual energy that will inspire and reward anyone who reads them.

Contagious Zeal. Bernard was born in 1090 or 1091 into a family of minor nobility in the French province of Burgundy. His father, Tescelin, was a knight, lord of the chateau of Fontaines on the outskirts of Dijon, and a godly man. His wife, Aleth of Montbard, was a devout woman, and together they raised their six sons (Bernard was the third) and one daughter to love God and the church.

The children grew up in the age of chivalry, their minds filled with tales of the crusaders and courtly songs of troubadours and minstrels. Bernard's older brothers and at least one of the younger were trained as knights, but Bernard's interests leaned more toward the academic. Showing great intellectual promise, he was sent to one of the most reputable schools in Burgundy.

Bernard was of medium stature but, because he was slender, he appeared taller. Blue-eyed, with a high forehead, bright blond hair and reddish beard, he had natural warmth and charm, a heart filled with charity, and the clear diction and eloquent gestures of a fine speaker. His classical studies trained him to be a remarkable thinker and Latin scholar, familiar with the works of Virgil, Ovid, and Cicero. However, when he was twenty-three, he decided to forego the life of a nobleman and scholar. In 1113, he entered Cîteaux, a monastery only a few miles from his family's castle.

Cîteaux had been established only fifteen years earlier, in 1098, while Bernard was a young boy. Called the "New Monastery," Cîteaux was not prestigious; rather, it was almost destitute. It had been founded by Robert of Molesme as a way to return monasticism to its roots by a stricter observance of the Rule of Saint Benedict. The monks of Cîteaux had initiated a reform movement not wholly popular among their more distinguished and richer Benedictine brothers.

So compelling was Bernard's anticipation of the life he was about to embrace that he managed to persuade thirty other noblemen, including his uncle, four of his brothers, a cousin, and friends, to join him. William of Saint Thierry, a contemporary of Bernard and his first biographer, wrote, "Mothers hid their sons when Bernard came near, and wives clung to their husbands to prevent them from going to hear him." As he was about to lose his sons to this new monastery, Tescelin advised them, "Be moderate. I know you: Nothing can restrain your zeal!"

As Bernard and his brothers departed, Guy, the oldest, told Nivard, the youngest, that the family estate would be his. "What?" he exclaimed with remarkable wisdom, "You take heaven and leave me the earth. The division is too unfair!" As soon as he was old enough, Nivard too became a novice at Cîteaux. Later, Tescelin himself joined the sons he had given to the Lord, receiving the habit from Bernard and dying as a lay brother at Clairvaux. Even Tescelin's daughter Humbeline entered a convent after an inspirational visit with Bernard.

The Young Abbot of Clairvaux. With the arrival of Bernard and his companions, new energy was breathed into the reforming efforts of Cîteaux. Over the next two years, Cîteaux's abbot, Stephen Harding, sent out groups of monks to establish three new monasteries. Along with Cîteaux, these became the foundation of the Cistercian Order. In 1115, he sent Bernard and twelve monks—Bernard's uncle and brothers among them—to Champagne. It was in this remote and desolate region, known as the "Valley of Bitterness," that they founded the monastery they preferred to call Clairvaux, or "Clear Valley." Bernard was only twenty-five years old, but Harding recognized his wisdom, passion, and leadership skills, which made him the logical choice to be abbot of a new foundation. Bernard was ordained to the priesthood and received his blessing as abbot from Bishop William of Champeaux.

During the early years at Clairvaux, Bernard suffered from severe stomach problems that continued to plague him for the rest of his life. All the monks endured the rigors of clearing the woods, building a monastery, and tilling the soil. Their austere diet consisted of bread and barley or millet, beech leaves and beechnuts, and roots.

In addition to these hardships, they occasionally suffered from Bernard's high standards and overzealous severity. Over time, the young abbot learned to temper his ways, maturing in mercy and humility and becoming more compassionate and understanding toward the frailties of human nature—at least toward his fellow monks' if not his own. Although at times he could be overbearing, heated in anger, and quick to judge, a reserve and shyness added a touch of modesty to his personality. A leader who learned how to exercise authority with love as well as firmness, Bernard easily won the affection and respect of his monks.

Expansion. Soon Clairvaux was filled with men eager to follow the monastic way of life. In 1118, Bernard sent out a band of monks to Châlon to establish Clairvaux's first daughterhouse. A year later, another group was sent to Dijon, and in 1121, a third group settled in Soisson. This rapid pace of growth continued throughout Bernard's thirty-five-year administration as abbot. By the end of his life he was responsible for having founded sixty-eight monasteries, stretching from Scandinavia to Portugal and from England and Ireland to central Europe, southern Italy, and Sardinia. These daughterhouses of Clairvaux produced another one hundred abbeys by the time of his death. In a large measure, the phenomenal expansion of the Cistercian Order during the twelfth century was due to Bernard's dynamism and spiritual vision.

Bernard's fervor attracted men from all walks of life to the monastic ideal. On one occasion, after Bernard preached to seminarians at the university in Paris, twenty-three of them followed him back to Clairvaux. Knights, clerics, and even repentant robbers and rogues were found among his monks. Henri, the brother of King Louis VII of France, came to Clairvaux to ask Bernard's advice on temporal matters, and suddenly abandoned his companions and entered the monastery.

In 1119 Bernard attended a meeting of the abbots of the Cistercian monasteries convened by Stephen

Harding of Cîteaux. Though he was not yet thirty years old, his thoughts on the revival of the primitive spirit of the Benedictine rule and on fervor in all the monastic orders received great attention and respect. There the abbots gave definite form to the constitutions of the Cistercian Order and the regulations of the "Charter of Charity," confirmed by Pope Callixtus II in December of the same year.

During the first ten years at Clairvaux, Bernard's main concern was to see to it that fellow monks there and in every new house he founded experienced a full conversion of life. These brothers were to be deeply rooted in Christ through personal prayer, the reading and study of Scripture, and the rhythm of Benedictine life expressed through the liturgy and work. Around 1124, at the request of an abbot from a neighboring Cistercian monastery, Bernard wrote the treatise *On the Steps of Humility and Pride.* For the monks of the Grand Chartreuse Abbey, Bernard wrote *Letter of Love*, which eventually became part of his famous treatise *On Loving God.*

Bernard's letters and treatises soon began to reach churchmen, statesmen, and friends of all classes outside the monastery, and as his monks spread throughout Europe, his influence and reputation grew as well. As Bernard was called upon to expand his teaching office, he wrote *On the Conduct and Duties of Bishops*, which was well received by those engaged in pastoral care. Another work of these early years was Bernard's *Apology*, addressed to William of Saint Thierry, in which he mediated the spirited exchange between the reforming Cistercians and the Benedictine monks of Cluny. Other treatises soon followed.

Away from Home. More and more, as Bernard was called upon to arbitrate in both church and political disagreements, he was drawn into the public arena and the affairs of the world. "God's business is mine!" he once exclaimed. "Nothing that concerns him is foreign to me." Because of his reputation for sanctity and his talent as a mediator, princes asked him to decide their disputes, bishops sought his opinion on problems involving their churches, and popes accepted his counsel. Moreover, he was invited to attend many church synods and councils. His life, he once wrote, was "overrun everywhere by anxieties, suspicions, and cares. There is scarcely an hour free from the crowd of discordant applicants, and the troubles and cares of their business. I have no power to stop their coming and cannot refuse to see them, and they do not leave me even time to pray."

It was the greatest paradox of his life: Bernard, who had sought the contemplative life with God, became one of the most traveled and active leaders of the twelfth-century church. Bernard's friend William of Saint Thierry termed the problem "a conflict in his heart between his great desire for souls and the desire to remain hidden from the attention of the world."

Bernard frequently pointed out that he was pressed into service by the leaders of the church, but he usually entered those situations with zest and even seemed to relish them keenly. As one commentator pointed out, "Bernard *would* have preferred to remain in the monastery, but on some level he was also energized by these outside involvements and the influence he was able to exert in situations."

In 1130, a schism broke out in the Roman church when two rival popes, Innocent II and Anacletus, were elected. The sovereigns of Europe took differing sides in the split, and the church and continent were divided over the issue. For eight years Bernard labored to rally the church hierarchy and secular rulers around Innocent, whom he judged to be the rightful pope, and reestablish unity. Much of this time he accompanied Innocent around Europe, with intermittent returns to Clairvaux. "My soul is sorrowful and will not be comforted until I return to you," he told his monks in a letter to them. "What consolation can there be for me in this evil hour, in this land of my exile? There are only yourselves. Wherever I am, your dear memory never leaves me. But for this very reason your absence is all the more hard to endure."

Troubled Times. It was in 1135, during the troubled times of the schism, that Bernard began writing his sermons on the Old Testament's Song of Songs. By the end of 1136, when he was called to

Rome for the third time, he had already drafted the first twenty-four sermons. After his return to Clairvaux in 1138, he revised these and then continued, on and off throughout the next eighteen years, to produce sixty-two more sermons. He was still working on them when he died in 1153, and had, in the eighty-six sermons he completed, only reached the beginning of the third chapter of the Old Testament book.

During these middle years of his life, Bernard frequently defended the faith against unorthodox views. He was wary of the emerging scholastic approach, in which reason was seen as the way to establish and prove spiritual truths, viewing it as a threat to faith and the integrity of the gospel. He engaged in a public dispute with the controversial teacher Peter Abelard for his exaltation of reason over revelation, and ultimately some of Abelard's teachings were condemned.

In 1145, the Latin Kingdom of Jerusalem was threatened by the Muslims, and the pope called on Bernard to promote a new crusade to protect the Holy Land from Arab invasion and to enlist the rulers of Europe and their armies in "the cause of Christ." The crusade, launched in 1147, ended in dismal failure the following year, partly due to an undisciplined army and misconduct among the crusaders. Nonetheless, it was Bernard who was severely criticized because he had seemed to promise success.

In reply, Bernard declared that he had trusted in God's mercy to bless a crusade undertaken in God's name, but that the army's sins had brought catastrophe. Yet, he cautioned: "Who could judge the true success or failure? How is it that the rashness of mortals dares to condemn what they cannot understand?" Finally, Bernard consoled himself that it was better for people to be angry with him than with God.

When a former monk of Clairvaux was elected to the papacy in 1145, Bernard wrote for his former pupil the treatise *On Consideration*. The document is a careful reflection on the duties of a pope and the members of the Roman curia as well as a meditation on the importance of self-knowledge and the contemplation of God. The large number of manuscript copies of this treatise still preserved in the

Vatican Library indicates that many popes, cardinals, and other prelates possessed the work, which was a forceful reminder of their mission. In 1959, Pope John XXIII confided in his diary, *Journal of a Soul*, that he had been reading selections from the treatise. "There could be nothing more suitable and useful for a poor pope like myself," he wrote, "and for any pope at any time."

Toward the end of his life, Bernard put together an enormous collection of his letters, more than five hundred of which have been preserved. His correspondence to bishops, emperors, statesmen, abbots, queens, countesses, and nuns reveals the vast scope of his relationships. Whether engaging in heated debate with opponents, encouraging those considering a monastic vocation, chastising kings, advising popes, or sending warm greetings and expressions of affection to his wide circle of friends, Bernard was an alert, lively, and thoughtful writer.

The Death of a Saint. In 1152 Bernard wrote to Pope Eugene that he was "dying by inches." Yet in the spring of the following year he rose from his sickbed at the request of the archbishop of Trier to mediate in a political dilemma. Successful in reconciling the citizens of Metz and the duke of Lorraine, he returned to Clairvaux, knowing that death was approaching.

Late that summer Bernard's fellow abbots and monks gathered at his bed, grieved that he was leaving them. He replied, "I know not to which I ought to yield—the love of my children, which urges me to stay here; or to the love of my God, which draws me to him."

On August 20, 1153, the tolling of the bells announced to the world the death of the great abbot Bernard. The funeral chant was intoned by the seven hundred monks of Clairvaux. The founder of Clairvaux was canonized by Pope Alexander III in 1174, just twenty-one years after his death.

Bernard had, as any man, his weaknesses, failings, and flaws as well as his strengths and gifts. In his early zeal, he had been too harsh with his monks. He was occasionally quick-tempered—some of his letters were dictated in the heat of his fiery anger. At times he was hasty in his judgments and narrow-minded in support of his own interests. A man steeped in the traditional theology of the Middle Ages, he was perhaps unfair in so strongly condemning the pioneers of scholastic theology, worried that they would undermine the nature of faith. Yet in all this, Bernard was a man of tremendous passion, insight, and energy. Above all, he was an ardent lover of God whose faults were not incompatible with the heroic virtue and generous sacrifices of a saint.

Lover of God. This passion for God—and Bernard's profound experience and knowledge of God's love for him and for all humankind—is at the heart of all his work. No matter what his topic or the concerns he was addressing, his perspective was shaped by this mutual love. It was the foundation and underpinning of all his convictions and actions. The selections in *Love Songs: Wisdom from Saint Bernard of Clairvaux* have been chosen to highlight this reality.

The reader will discover in this book the major themes that flowed from this love: Bernard's hope and zeal to draw others into an understanding and experience of the love he had tasted; the centrality of Jesus' Incarnation and the salvation and mercy that is ours through Christ; an ever-deepening conversion and transformation in Christ that is the only fully appropriate response to be made to that love; a profound honor and appreciation for Mary, the virgin mother of Christ; and finally, prayer and desire for union with the Beloved. Excerpts have been taken from:

～ *On Loving God,* the best known of Bernard's treatises. In this work, he speaks of the four steps of love: from self-love, to love of God for the sake of what he has done for us, then to loving God for his sake alone, and finally, to loving ourselves for God's sake. This journey is made possible because of God's mercy. Bernard shows that the whole reason for our existence is to love God, and until we love him, we have not really begun to live. We love God not as a slave obeying a master out of fear of punishment, but as sons and daughters who are heirs of a loving and generous Father.

∽ *Sermons on the Song of Songs*, Bernard's literary masterpiece. The Old Testament's Song of Songs was particularly popular in the Middle Ages, at a time when spirituality and a focus on personal experience flourished. In Bernard's day, more than thirty commentaries on the Song were in circulation, all of them interpreting the text in light of God's passionate, unquenchable love for the church and the individual soul. Bernard drew a portrait of the soul as the bride in love with the divine Bridegroom and their union with one another.

∽ *Liturgical sermons*, which form a commentary on the liturgical year. The sermons begin with Advent and move through the main events in the life of Christ and mysteries of salvation as well as the major saints' days celebrated throughout the church year. Many of these sermons were composed solely for reading and publication, while others Bernard actually preached to his monks.

◇ *On the Steps of Humility and Pride*, an early treatise written to help Bernard's monks "ascend" the ladder of humility and at the same time "descend" the steps of pride. The goal of this labor, he stressed, is knowledge of the truth.

◇ *In Praise of the Virgin Mother*, written while Bernard was convalescing from an illness and reflecting on Luke's Gospel of the Annunciation. These four sermons, addressed to his monks, point to Mary's unique role in God's plan of redemption with a freshness that reveals Bernard's deep devotion to her and his reliance on her intercession.

◇ *In Praise of the New Knighthood*, a treatise written to guide and inspire the Knights Templar, a new religious order established by the church to protect pilgrims and other Christians in the Holy Land.

◇ *The Parables* and *The Sentences*, a collection of Bernard's sayings and homilies. Some of these have been preserved only in the form of a summary by those who listened to him. Other notes taken by his hearers provide the sentence-by-sentence development of his actual text. These notes convey the oral style Bernard excelled in as surely as his published works convey his prose style.

∿ *On Conversion*, a public discourse on "conversion of heart" given to scholars and students in Paris, probably in 1140, in order to attract them to the monastic life.

∿ *On Consideration*, written for his former monk, Pope Eugene III, enumerating the duties of the papacy.

Drawing Honey from Scripture. All of Bernard's writings are rooted in Scripture. His own life and prayer were nourished and shaped by the language of the Bible, and his works breathe of his familiarity with it. Scripture verses and the thoughts of the Fathers of the Church, whose writings he also knew thoroughly, filled his mind and memory and overflowed spontaneously into his sermons and theological commentaries.

In the monastic tradition, monks are not only to read God's word, but to taste it, chew on it, digest it—drawing from it sweetness and life. Bernard once described this way of prayerfully meditating on Scripture: "As food is sweet to the palate, so does a psalm delight the heart. But those who are sincere and wise will not fail to 'chew' the psalm with their minds. If they 'swallow' it in a lump, without properly chewing it, the palate will be cheated of the delicious flavor, sweeter even than honey that drips from the comb."

Formally declared a Doctor of the Church in 1830, Bernard has been given the title "Doctor Mellifluous" because of his interpretations of Scripture. The term "mellifluous," meaning "sweetly flowing," as with honey, was already applied to him not long after his death because he was so able to draw "honey"—the richness and sweetness of the spiritual or hidden meaning—out of the literal sense of the Scripture as if drawing honey from the comb. Many of the oldest artworks and images of Bernard show him writing or holding an open Bible, displaying it as he comments on it, initiating the "flow" of mystical doctrine. Honeybees and writing pens are two symbols associated with Bernard.

From the Distance of a Millennium. Written so many years ago, Bernard's works naturally display many of the genres and styles common to the twelfth century. In order to bridge the centuries, and to make your experience with Bernard more enjoyable and rewarding, a few words of orientation are helpful:

∼ Bernard lived in and was shaped by a different age and culture than ours. His favorite and typical way of writing and preaching was to "unpack" a Scripture text through a running commentary rich with allusions, rhetorical and poetic imagery, and word plays. His use of allegory and symbolism in his approach to explaining Scripture may be foreign to the modern reader, but was customary to the medieval mind. Often it may seem that he gave free rein to his imagination and found allegorical meanings in the text that today appear more poetic and cleverly inventive than strictly theological.

However, we must realize that while some of Bernard's allegories may strike us as extravagant or as a "far stretch" from the text, he also recognized the underlying literal meaning of the text and could be confident that his listeners did as well. His figurative treatment and biblical "word games" do not indicate a lack of interest in the true meaning of the words, but rather presuppose a thorough and complete knowledge of it. Take care that these stylistic features do not distract you from recognizing the value and richness of Bernard's thought and of his human and spiritual experiences.

∾ Bernard wrote in Latin, and much of his elegant prose is very poetic in its use of rhyme, alliteration, assonance, and refined sense of rhythm. His choice of words and his phrasing were vivid, animated, and smooth. Unfortunately, any translation, no matter how carefully done, loses some of the beauty and harmony in Bernard's original text. We have sought to use the best translations available when choosing the selections for *Love Songs: Wisdom from Saint Bernard of Clairvaux*.

In order to make these writings more accessible to the modern reader, *The Word Among Us Press* was kindly granted permission by Cistercian Publications to make minor adaptations in the translations where this would make the English more readable today. We want to give special thanks to Cistercian Publications for allowing us to adapt this material. If you would like to explore more of Bernard's writings and his life, we have included suggestions for further reading at the end of the book.

While Bernard's style may challenge the modern reader, his words and ideas are not outdated or irrelevant. Though nearly a millennium old, they have maintained their vitality and they speak to the deepest desires and longings of every age: the desire of the human heart to be fully united to

God. May your efforts to know the mind and heart and soul of the great abbot of Clairvaux, be rewarded with that union.

Jeanne Kun
Editor

Love Beyond Measure

No Limit to Loving

You wish me to tell you why and how God should be loved. My answer is that God himself is the reason why he should be loved. As for how he is to be loved, there is to be no limit to that love.

There are two reasons why God should be loved for his own sake: No one can be loved more justly and no one can be loved with greater benefit. Indeed, when we ask, why should God be loved, we may mean, why does God deserve our love? Or we may mean, what will we gain by loving God? My answer to both questions is assuredly the same, for I can see no other reason for loving God except for himself. So let us first see how he deserves our love.

God certainly deserves a lot from us since he gave himself to us when we did not deserve it at all (Galatians 1:4). Besides, what could he have given us that is better than himself? So, when questioning why

God should be loved, if we ask what right he has to be loved, the answer is that the main reason for loving him is that "He loved us first" (1 John 4:19). Surely he is worthy of being loved in return when we think of who loves, whom he loves, and how much he loves.

God's love is genuine, for it is the love of One who does not seek his own advantage (1 Corinthians 13:5). To whom is such love shown? It is written: "While we were still his enemies, he reconciled us to himself" (Romans 5:10). Thus God loved freely, and even when we were enemies. How much did he love? St. John answers that: "God so loved the world that he gave his only-begotten Son" (John 3:16). St. Paul adds: "He did not spare his only Son, but delivered him up for us" (Romans 8:32). The Son also said of himself: "No one has greater love than he who lays down his life for his friends" (John 15:13). Thus the righteous One deserves to be loved by the wicked, the highest and omnipotent One by the weak. ༄

Chapter One
On Loving God

I Will Love You As
Much As I Can

Consider first how God deserves to be loved, that there is to be no limit to that love, for he loved us first (1 John 4:10). He loved us so much and so freely, insignificant as we are and such as we are, that, as you recall I said in the beginning, we must love God without any limit. Finally—since God is both infinite and immeasurable—what, I ask, should be the aim or degree of our love? What about the fact that our love is not given gratuitously but in payment of a debt? Thus the Immeasurable loves, the Eternal loves, that Charity which surpasses knowledge loves (Ephesians 3:19). God, whose greatness knows no end (Psalm 145:3), to whose wisdom there is no limit (Psalm 147:5), whose peace exceeds all understanding (Philippians 4:7), loves—and we think we can repay him with some measure of love?

My God, my help, I will love you as much as I am able for your gift. My love is less than you deserve, yet not less than I am able, for even if I cannot love you as much as I should, still I cannot love you more than

I can. I will only be able to love you more when you give me more, although you can never find my love worthy of you. For, "Your eyes have seen my imperfections, and all shall be written down in your book" (Psalm 139:16), all who do what they can, even if they cannot do all they should. As far as I can see, it is clear enough to what extent God ought to be loved, and to that extent because he deserves it. ❧

Chapter Six
On Loving God

THE FOUR DEGREES OF LOVE

A person first loves himself for himself because he is carnal and sensitive to nothing but himself. Then, when he sees he cannot exist by himself, he begins to seek God by faith (Hebrews 11:6) and to love God as something necessary for his own welfare. So in the second degree of love, man loves God for his own sake and not for God's sake. When forced by his own needs, he begins to honor God and care for him by thinking of him, reading about him, praying to him, and obeying him. God reveals himself gradually in this kind of familiarity and consequently becomes lovable.

When man tastes how sweet God is (Psalm 34:8), he passes to the third degree of love in which he loves God now not because of his own needs but because of God. No doubt a person remains a long time in this degree, and I doubt if he ever attains the fourth degree during this life— that is, if he ever loves only for God's sake. Let those who have had the experience let me know; to me, I confess, it seems impossible. No doubt, this happens when the good and faithful servant is introduced into his Lord's joy (Matthew 25:21), and is overwhelmed by the richness of God's dwelling (Psalm 36:8). In some wondrous way he forgets himself. Then, ceasing to belong to himself, he passes entirely into God, and clinging to him, he becomes one with him in spirit (1 Corinthians 6:17). ❧

Chapter Fifteen
On Loving God

A CHILD OR A SLAVE?

We can acknowledge that the Lord is powerful, that the Lord is good to us, and that the Lord is simply good. The first view is the love of a slave who fears for himself; the second is that of a hired worker who thinks only of himself; the third is that of a son who honors his father. He, therefore, who fears and he who covets do so for themselves. Genuine love is found only in the son. It does not seek its own advantage (1 Corinthians 13:5).

Love alone can turn the mind away from loving ourselves and the world and fix it on loving God. Neither fear nor love of self can change the soul. At times they change our appearance or deeds, but they can never alter our character. Sometimes even a slave can do God's work, but it is not done freely; he is still in bondage. The hired worker can do it also, but not freely; he is seen to be motivated by his own greed. Let the slave have his own law, the very fear which binds him (Romans 2:14). Let the hired worker's be the lust for gain which restrains him when he is attracted and enticed by temptation (James 1:14). But neither of these is without fault nor can either convert souls. Love converts us because it makes us act willingly.

Love is the divine substance. I am saying nothing new or unusual, just what St. John says: "God is love" (1 John 4:8). Therefore, it is rightly said, love is God, and the gift of God (Ephesians 2:8). Thus love leads to love; genuine love produces the quality of love. ∞

Chapter Twelve
On Loving God

THE BRIDE'S REQUEST

If a love relationship is the special and outstanding characteristic of the bride and groom, it is appropriate to call the person who loves God a bride. Now a woman who asks for a kiss is in love. It is not for liberty that she asks, nor for a present, not for an inheritance nor even knowledge, but for a kiss. It is the request of a bride who is chaste, who breathes forth a love that is holy, a love whose ardor she cannot entirely disguise. . . . With a spontaneous outburst from the abundance of her heart (Matthew 12:34), direct even to the point of boldness, she says: "Let him kiss me with the kiss of his mouth" (Song of Songs 1:2).

Her love is surely pure when she pursues the person she loves, and not some other thing that he can give to her. It is a holy love, the impulse of an upright spirit rather than of physical desire. And it is burning love, blinded by its own ardor to the majesty of the beloved. . . . How great this power of love: what great confidence and freedom of spirit! What is more clear than that fear is driven out by perfect love (1 John 4:18)! ❧

Sermon Seven
On the Song of Songs I

LEARN FROM CHRIST HOW TO LOVE

Christian, learn from Christ how you should love Christ. Learn a love that is tender, wise, strong. Love with tenderness, not passion; wisdom, not foolishness; and strength, lest you become weary and turn away from the love of the Lord. Do not let the glory of the world or the pleasure of the flesh lead you astray; the wisdom of Christ should become sweeter to you than these. The light of Christ should shine so much for you that the spirit of lies and deceit will not seduce you. Finally, Christ, as the strength of God, should support you so that you may not be worn down by difficulties (1 Corinthians 1:24).

Let love enkindle your zeal, let knowledge animate it, let faithfulness strengthen it. Keep your love fervent, discreet, and courageous. See it is not lukewarm or timid. See for yourself if those three commands are not prescribed in the law when God says: "You shall love the Lord your God with your whole heart, your whole soul, and your whole strength" (Deuteronomy 6:5). It seems to me, if no more suitable meaning for this triple distinction comes to mind, that the love of the heart relates to a certain warmth of affection, the love of the soul to the energy or judgment of reason, and the love of strength can refer to faithfulness and vigor of spirit. So love the Lord your God with the full and deep affection of your heart; love him with your mind wholly awake and enlightened; love him with all your strength, so much so that you would not even fear to die for love of him. ❧

Sermon Twenty
On the Song of Songs I

REWARDS OF LOVING GOD

God is not loved without a reward, although he should be loved without regard for one. True love cannot be worthless. Still, as "it does not seek its own advantage" (1 Corinthians 13:5), it cannot be considered mercenary. Love pertains to the will, it is not a transaction; it cannot acquire or be acquired by a pact. Moving us freely, it makes us spontaneous. True love is content with itself; it has its reward, but that reward is the object that we love. Whatever you seem to love because of something else, you do not really love; you really love the end pursued and not that by which it is pursued.

True love deserves its reward, it does not seek it. A reward is offered to him who does not yet love; it is due to him who does love; it is given to him who perseveres. When we have to persuade people in lesser affairs, we cajole the unwilling with promises and rewards, not those who are willing. Who would dream of offering a man a reward for doing something he wants to do? No one, for example, pays a hungry man to eat, a thirsty man to drink, or a mother to feed the child of her womb (Isaiah 49:15). Who would think of using prayers or prizes to remind a man to fence in his vine, to dig around his tree, or to build his own home? How much more the person who loves God seeks no other reward than the God whom he loves. Were that person to demand anything else, then he would certainly love that other thing and not God.

I said earlier that God is the reason for loving God. That is right, for he is the final cause of our love. He offers the opportunity, creates the affection, and fulfills the desire. He makes, or rather is made himself lovable. He hopes to be so happily loved that he will not be loved in vain. His love prepares and rewards ours (1 John 4:19). Graciously he leads the way; reasonably he repays us; for he is our sweet hope. Rich for all who call on him (Romans 10:12), although he can give us nothing better than himself. He gave himself to merit for us; he keeps himself to be our reward; he serves himself as food for us; he sold himself in ransom for the captives.

O Lord, you are so good to those who seek you (Lamentations 3:25)! What must you be to those who find you? More wonderful still, no one can seek you unless he has already found you. You wish to be found that you may be sought for, and sought for to be found. ❧

Chapters Six and Seven
On Loving God

THE CREATOR OF EVERYTHING GOOD

In order to love our neighbor with perfect justice, we must look to God. In other words, how can we love our neighbor with purity, if we do not love him in God? But it is impossible to love in God unless we love God. It is necessary, therefore, to love God first. Then we can love our neighbor in God (Mark 12:31). Thus God makes himself lovable and creates whatever else is good.

God does it this way. He who made nature sustains it, for nature was created in such a way that its Maker is its protector forever. The world could not exist without him. So that we do not ignore this fact or dare to claim through pride what God has done, our wise Father has decided to discipline us by our trials. Then, when we fail and God comes to our aid, we who are saved by God will give him the glory that is due him. It is written: "Call to me in the day of sorrows; I will deliver you, and you shall honor me" (Psalm 50:15). In this way, we who are unspiritual human beings (1 Corinthians 2:14) and know how to love only ourselves, will start loving God for his own benefit, because we learn from frequent experience that we can do everything that is good for us in God (Philippians 4:13), and that without God, we can do nothing good (John 15:5). ❧

Chapter Eight
On Loving God

THE EMBRACE

Be imitators of God, like dear children, and walk in love, as Christ also has loved you (Ephesians 5:1-2). Such a likeness weds us to the Word, for one who is like the Word by nature shows himself like him too in what he does, loving as he is loved. When we love perfectly, we are wedded to the Word. What is lovelier than conforming ourselves to Christ? What is more desirable than love, by which we, not content with a human master, approach the Word with confidence, cling to him faithfully, speak to him as a familiar friend, and refer to him in every matter with an intellectual grasp equal to the boldness of our desires? Truly this is a spiritual contract, a holy marriage. It is more than a contract, it is an embrace: an embrace where identity of will makes of two one spirit (1 Corinthians 6:17).

There need be no fear that inequality between God and ourselves should hinder us in conforming our will to his, because love is no respecter of persons. It is from loving, not revering, that love receives its name. Let someone filled with horror or stupor or fear or wonder be content with reverence;

where there is love all these are unimportant. Love is sufficient for itself; when love is present it absorbs and conquers all other affections. Therefore it loves what it loves, and it knows nothing else. He who is justly honored, held in awe, and admired, prefers to be loved. God and the soul are Bridegroom and Bride. What other bond or compulsion do we look for between those who are betrothed, except to love and be loved? ⮀

Sermon Eighty-three
On the Song of Songs IV

FOR NO OTHER REASON

Love is the only one of the inspirations of the soul, of its senses and affections, in which the creature can respond to its Creator—even if not as an equal—and repay his favor in some similar way. For example, if God is angry with me, am I to be angry in return? No, indeed, but I will tremble with fear (Job 26:11) and ask pardon. So also, if he accuses me, I will not accuse him in return, but rather justify him. Nor, if he judges me, will I judge him, but I will adore him. In saving me, he does not ask to be saved by me; nor does he who sets all men free, need to be set free by me. If he commands, I must obey, and not demand his service or obedience.

Now you see how different love is, for when God loves, he desires nothing but to be loved. Since he loves us for no other reason than to be loved, he knows that those who love him are blessed in their very love. ⁓

Sermon Eighty-three
On the Song of Songs IV

THE HEIGHT AND DEPTH, THE BREADTH AND LENGTH

God should be loved perfectly by each of us, and should be feared as well. He should be feared because God is that power which no one can resist (2 Chronicles 20:6) and that wisdom which no one can flee. Moreover, he should be loved because he is himself that charity (1 John 4:8) which loves us, and there should be no doubt about his love for us.

God is the one who does not deceive anyone—he is truth, and so he loves truthfully. So anyone who fears and loves God perfectly can understand what is God's height and depth, breadth and length (Ephesians 3:18). His height is his power; his depth his wisdom, which encompasses all things; his width his charity; and his length his truth—this is the same thing as his eternity, which is without either beginning or end, just like his truth. ❧

The Parables and The Sentences

2

Jesus Christ, True God and True Man

AT THE NAME OF JESUS

The name of Jesus is more than light, it is also food. Do you not feel greater strength as often as you remember it? What other name can so enrich us when we meditate on it? What can equal its power to refresh our harassed senses, to build up godly virtues, to add vigor to good and upright habits, to foster pure affections? Every food of the mind is dry if it is not dipped in that oil; it is tasteless if not seasoned by that salt. Write what you will, I shall not relish it if you exclude the name of Jesus. Jesus to me is honey in the mouth, music in the ear, a song in the heart.

Again, it is like medicine. Do you feel sad? (James 5:13). Let the name of Jesus come into your heart. From there let it spring to your mouth, so that shining like the dawn it may dispel all darkness and make a cloudless sky. Does someone fall into sin? Does his despair even urge him to suicide? Let him but cry out this life-giving name and his will to live will be at once renewed. The hardness of heart that is our common experience, the apathy bred of laziness, bitterness of mind, repulsion for the things of the spirit—have they ever failed to yield in presence of that saving name? The tears dammed up by the barrier of our pride—how have they not burst forth again with sweeter abundance at the thought of Jesus' name?

And where is the person, who, terrified and trembling before impending danger, has not been suddenly filled with courage and rid of fear by calling on the strength of Jesus' name? Where is the man who, tossed on the rolling sea of doubt, did not quickly find certainty by the clarity of Jesus' name? Was anyone ever so discouraged, so beaten down by afflictions, to whom the sound of this name did not bring new resolve? In short, for all the ills and disorders which we suffer, the name of Jesus is medicine. For proof we have no less than his own promise: "Call upon me in the day of trouble; I will deliver you, and you shall glorify me" (Psalm 50:15).

Nothing so curbs the onset of anger, so allays the upsurge of pride. It cures the wound of envy, controls unbridled extravagance, and quenches the flame of lust. It cools the thirst of greed and banishes the itch of unclean desire. For when I name Jesus, I set before me a man who is meek and humble of heart (Matthew 11:29), kind, prudent, chaste, merciful, flawlessly upright, and holy in the eyes of all. This same man is the all-powerful God whose way of life heals me, whose support is my strength. All these re-echo for me at the hearing of Jesus' name. Because he is man I strive to imitate him; because of his divine power I lean upon him. The examples of his human life I gather like medicinal herbs; with the aid of his power I blend them, and the result is a compound like no pharmacist can produce.

Hidden as in a vase, in this name of Jesus, you, my soul, possess a healthy remedy against which no spiritual illness will be proof. Carry it always close to your heart, always in your hand, and so ensure that all your affections, all your actions, are directed to Jesus.

The name of Jesus furnishes the power to correct your evil actions and to supply what is lacking in perfection. In this name your affections find a guard against corruption, or if corrupted, a power that will make them whole again. ∾

Sermon Fifteen
On the Song of Songs I

YOUR SINS ARE FORGIVEN

See Jesus instructing the disciples on the mountain by his words (Matthew 5:2) at the same time that he enlightens heaven's angels in silence. See how at the touch of his hand a leper is healed (8:3), blindness dispelled (9:29-30), the deaf are empowered to hear, the dumb to speak (Mark 7:33-35), the sinking disciple is rescued on the lake (Matthew 14:31). You will surely recognize him as the one to whom David long ago uttered the words: "You opened your hand, you satisfy the desire of every living thing" (Psalm 145:16); and again: "When you open your hand, all are filled with your goodness" (Psalm 104:28).

See how, prostrate at his feet, the penitent finds assurance as she is told: "Your sins are forgiven" (Luke 7:48). She knows that he is the one written about long ago: "The devil shall go forth before his feet" (Habakkuk 3:5, Vulgate). For when sin is forgiven, it is certain that the devil is driven out from the sinner's heart, and for this reason Christ embraced all sinners: "Now judgment is being passed on this world, now the prince of this world is overthrown" (John 12:31). God removes our sin when we make a humble confession, and thereby the devil loses the sovereignty he had gained over our hearts. ❧

Sermon Six
On the Song of Songs I

THE FRAGRANCE OF TRUTH

At Christ's conception there streamed from the fullness of the overshadowing Spirit (Luke 1:35) a shaft of heavenly brightness so blinding that not even the holy Virgin could have endured it had not the power of the Spirit given her shade. His birth radiated through the purity of his mother. His life was aflame with innocence, his teaching with truth, his miracles with purity of heart, his sacraments with the hidden power of his goodness. His passion shone with his acceptance of suffering, his death with the freedom he had to avoid death, his resurrection with the radiance which gave fortitude to the martyrs, his ascension with the glory of promises fulfilled.

How splendid also is the fragrance of faith in all these mysteries! That faith is ours, and fills our hearts and minds, although we have not seen their radiance! "Blessed are those who have not seen, yet have believed" (John 20:29). May my part in these mysteries be the fragrance of my life which flows from them. It is through faith that I breathe in their fragrance. Indeed, these truths are so great that they lighten the burden of my exile here on earth, and ever renew in my heart the longing for my true home in heaven. ◌

Sermon Seventy
On the Song of Songs IV

HE SOUGHT ME OUT

Our Savior's love was sweet, and wise, and strong. I call it sweet because he took on a human body, wise because he avoided sin, strong because he endured death. Even though he took a body, his love was never sensual but always in the wisdom of the Spirit. . . . Those whom he sought after in a body, he loved in the spirit and redeemed in power.

How sweet it is to see as man the Creator of humanity. While he carefully protected nature from sin, he forcefully drove death from that nature also. In taking a body he stooped to me, in avoiding sin he took counsel with himself, in accepting death he satisfied the Father. A dear friend, a wise counselor, a strong helper. Should I not willingly entrust myself to the One who had the good will, the wisdom, and the strength to save me? He sought me out, he called me through grace (Romans 8:30). Will he refuse me as I come to him? ◡

Sermon Twenty
On the Song of Songs I

CLOTHED IN HUMANITY

In the Lord's Coming, if I consider who it is who comes, I cannot grasp his greatness. If I consider to whom he comes, I shrink in awe because he lowered himself for us. The angels, openly ascending and descending upon the Son of man, must surely marvel to behold him lower than themselves (Hebrews 2:7), whom always they adore as over them. If I consider why he came, then I embrace, so far as I am able, the unthinkable scope of his love. And if I think about the way in which he came, I recognize how noble is humanity's rank (Psalm 8:5). The Creator and Lord of the universe came in truth; he came to men, he came from men, he came as man.

But somebody will say, "How can we say he *came*, when he was always there?" He was in the world indeed, and the world was made by him; but the world knew him not (John 1:10). So he did not come, as One who formerly was absent. He appeared, rather, as One who previously was hid. He who dwells in light to which no man can approach (1 Timothy 6:16) took on human form so that in it men might know him. And it was surely not beneath him for our Majesty to let himself be seen in his own likeness, which he made in the beginning. Nor was it an unworthy thing for God to be shown in the image of those who lacked the power to know him as he is. So when God, who had made man in his own image and likeness (Genesis 1:26), was himself made man, he was made known to men.

Sermon on the Advent of the Lord

TRUE GOD AND TRUE MAN

O mighty, marvelous mystery! The Child is circumcised and he is called Jesus (Luke 2:21). How are the two related? For circumcision seems a thing not for the Savior but for him who needs salvation. The Savior's part is surely to perform the circumcision, not to suffer it. But you must recognize in Jesus the mediator between God and man (1 Timothy 2:5), who from the outset of his birth associates things human with the very loftiest of things divine. He is born of a woman (Galatians 4:4), but of one whose fruitfulness so comes to her that her virginity remains intact. He is wrapped in swaddling clothes (Luke 2:7), and yet those very clothes are honored by the angel's praise (2:12). He is hidden in a manger (2:7), but a star in heaven makes him known (Matthew 2:2).

In the same way his circumcision proves that it is genuine manhood that he has assumed; and the Name that is above every name (Philippians 2:9) declares the glory of his majesty. He is circumcised as a true son of Abraham; he is called Jesus as a true Son of God. For my Jesus, unlike others who have been so called, does not bear the name in vain. The Evangelist tells us that he was called Jesus before he was conceived in the womb (Luke 2:31); and now, here, after his birth, he is called Jesus by everyone. For he is the Savior of both angels and humanity—of men and women from the time of his Incarnation, but of angels from the beginning of creation. ∾

Sermon on the Circumcision of the Lord

THE KEEN EYES OF FAITH

The Magi came from the East, where the sun rises (Matthew 2:1), to seek the risen Sun of Righteousness (Malachi 4:2). At a new star's leading (Matthew 2:9), they worshipped him to whom the Virgin had just given birth (2:11). They called him God, not with their lips but by their deeds. Whatever are you doing, you Magi? You worship a baby at the breast, in a poor shed, in common swaddling clothes! Is he then God? God is in his holy temple

(Psalm 11:4); the Lord's seat is in heaven (Psalm 2:4); yet you are looking for him in a wretched stable and on his mother's lap! What do you mean by offering him gold (Matthew 2:11)? Is he a king? If so, where is his palace, where is his throne, and where are the many members of a royal court? Is the stable a palace? Is the manger a throne? Do Joseph and Mary constitute a court?

Behold how clearly faith sees! Consider carefully what keen eyes it has! It knows the Son of God in a sucking babe, it knows him hanging on a cross, it knows him as he dies. For the Magi knew him in the stable, wrapped in swaddling clothes (Matthew 2:10); the thief recognized him on the cross, pierced with nails (Luke 23:40-42); and the centurion acknowledged Life in death (Mark 15:39). The first two saw the power of God in extreme bodily weakness; the last one saw the Highest Spirit in the yielding of his breath (John 19:30). The Magi see the Word of God in wordless babyhood, and witness by their gifts to the faith that the others express in words. The thief proclaims him King, and the centurion says that he is both man and the Son of God—exactly what the Magi's own three gifts declare, except that their incense shows him to be God, rather than Son of God. ❧

Sermon on the Epiphany of the Lord

LORD AND SON OF DAVID

T*he angel Gabriel was sent from God into a city of Galilee named Nazareth* (Luke 1:26). Are you surprised that Nazareth, a little city, should receive the honor of a visit from the herald of so great a King, and such a herald too? Ah, but a great treasure lies hidden (Matthew 13:44) in this little place, hidden from everyone, that is, but not from God. Is not Mary God's treasure? His heart is with her, wherever she is (6:21). His eyes are on her; all the time he looks upon the lowliness of his handmaiden (Luke 1:48).

The Father's sole-begotten Son knows heaven, does he not? Well, if he knows heaven, he knows Nazareth too. How should he not know his own fatherland? How should he not acknowledge his inheritance? As the Son of his Father, he claims heaven as his own by right. As the son of his mother, he claims Nazareth, even as he declares himself to be both Lord and Son of David (Mark 12:37). "The heaven of heavens is the Lord's: the earth has he given to the children of men" (Psalm 115:16). Both must acknowledge him their Owner, because he is not only Lord but also Son of man. ∽

Sermon on the Annunciation

3

Salvation and Mercy

EMPTIED FOR OUR SAKE

Christ's self-emptying was neither a simple gesture nor a limited one. He emptied himself even to the assuming of human nature, even to accepting death, death on a cross (Philippians 2:7). Who is there that can adequately gauge the greatness of the humility, gentleness, and self-surrender, revealed by the Lord of majesty in assuming human nature, in accepting the punishment of death, the shame of the cross? But somebody will say: "Surely the Creator could have restored his original plan without all that hardship?" Yes, he could, but he chose the way of personal suffering so that man would never again have a reason to display that worst and most hateful of all vices, ingratitude.

Even if God made you out of nothing, you have not been redeemed out of nothing. In six days he created all things, and among them, you. On the other hand, for a period of thirty whole years he worked your salvation in the midst of the earth. What he endured in those labors! To his bodily needs and the abuses from his enemies did he not add the mightier burden of the humiliation of the cross, and crown it all with the horror of his death? And this was indeed necessary. Man and beast you save, O Lord (Psalm 36:6). How you have multiplied your mercy, O God! ❧

Sermon Eleven
On the Song of Songs I

CHRIST RESTORES OUR LIFE

How do we know that Christ is able to forgive sins? No doubt it is because he is God and can do whatever he wishes. But how do we know that he is God? It is proved by his miracles. He did things which nobody else was able to do (John 15:24), not to mention the predictions of the prophets (Isaiah 9:6) and the voice of the Father coming down to him from the majestic glory of heaven (2 Peter 1:17; Matthew 17:5). If God be with us, who is against us? (Romans 8:31). It is God who justifies; who can condemn? (8:33-34). If it is he and none other to whom we daily confess, "Against you alone have I sinned" (Psalm 51:4), who better, or rather who else, can forgive what has been done against him alone? How could he not be able to forgive sins, who is able to do all things (Wisdom 7:27; Matthew 28:18)? If I can forgive an offense against me at will, cannot God, too, acquit the offenses we commit against him? If then the Almighty and he alone against whom we have sinned can forgive sins (Luke 5:21), blessed are they whose sins the Lord does not hold against them (Psalm 32:2). Therefore we know that Christ can cancel sin by the power of his divinity.

And who can doubt that he is ready to do so? How could he refuse us his justice when he assumed our flesh and even endured our death? He freely took flesh, freely suffered, and was freely crucified. Why then should he withhold only the gift of justification? Just as he is plainly able to forgive sin because he is divine, so he is evidently willing to forgive sin because of his humanity. ❧

In Praise of the New Knighthood

REDEEMED BY HIS BLOOD

To redeem a servant, the Father spares not his own Son, and the Son delivers himself up most willingly. Both send the Holy Spirit, and the Spirit himself intercedes for us with unspeakable groanings (Romans 8:26).

O hard, and hardened, and hard-hearted children of Adam! How can you remain unmoved by such great kindness, such blazing fire, so prodigious a flame of love, and so ardent a lover, who paid such an extravagant price for a worthless piece of goods? "Not with perishable things like gold and silver" did Jesus redeem us, but with his own "precious blood" (1 Peter 1:18-19) which flowed out liberally from the five parts of Jesus' body. What more should he have done that he did not do? He enlightened the blind, brought back the stragglers, reconciled the guilty, and justified the ungodly. Thirty-three years he was seen on earth. He lived among humans, he died for humans, he spoke concerning the Cherubim and Seraphim and all the angelic powers and they came to be (Psalm 33:9). When he wills it, all power is there with him (Wisdom 12:18).

What then does he who sought you with such concern now seek from you, if not that you walk mindfully with your God (Micah 6:8)? No one but the Holy Spirit enables us to this. It is he who probes the depth of our hearts (1 Corinthians 2:10), he who discerns the thoughts and intentions of the heart (Hebrews 4:12). He does not allow the slightest amount of chaff to settle inside the dwelling of a heart which he possesses, but consumes it in an instant with a fire of the most minute scrutiny. He is the sweet and gentle Spirit who bends our will, or rather straightens and directs it more fully toward his own so that we may be able to understand his will truly, love it fervently, and fulfill it effectively. ❧

Pentecost, Sermon Two

ON THE RECOVERY OF THE HUMAN
RACE, WHICH WAS LOST

As a result of Mercy's effort, an assembly was held in the heavenly recesses of God to recover the fallen human race. In this council Mercy and Truth met with each other (Psalm 85:10). When two people meet with one another, each must approach the other in order that they may meet; otherwise they do not come together. If Mercy did not meet Truth, she would be not mercy, but misery. If Truth did not meet with Mercy, she would be not verity, but severity.

So here Mercy and Truth met with one another, and Mercy discussed the damnation of the human race with Truth. Truth said: "The judgment has been fixed. The human race is dead. For Adam was told: 'In the hour when you eat of it, you will surely die' (Genesis 2:17). He did not obey; he ate. He is surely dead."

Mercy replied: "Must it be that one who is sleeping will never rise again? What if a human being without sin were created from the same earth? Perhaps he could wipe out the sin of the first human?"

But Truth responded: "Impossible! For the earth

is accursed in the work of Adam and it will yield him nothing but brambles and thistles" (Genesis 3:17-18).

Then Mercy said: "Certainly, the earth is accursed insofar as Adam's work is concerned, but is it in terms of ours? And so it may be possible for a human being without sin to be created from it."

"Recall humanity and the angels," replied Truth. "Remember that each of them has fallen, and recall that, without exception, every human being is but a shadow (Psalm 39:6). How could it be that a single human being, to whom the role of saving the whole world will be given, would not simply prove powerless? For to save is a greater thing than to be created, and it must be feared that one who was not faithful in small matters is unlikely to be found faithful in a great one" (Luke 19:17).

Mercy responded: "It is true, Truth, that every human being is but a shadow. But if you, steadfast Truth, were willing to undertake the task, no hint of vanity would undermine your effort."

At this Truth exclaimed: "Father, let this cup pass from me, if it is possible. Nonetheless, let it be not as I will, but as you wish" (Matthew 26:39).

Justice, hearing these words, intervened, saying: "Impossible. The scepter of our kingdom is the scepter of integrity (Psalm 45:6). In the realm of justice, no sin can remain unpunished. Mercy cannot join with truth, nor truth with mercy."

But Truth again exclaimed: "Father, if it is not possible for this cup to pass from me unless I drink of it, let your will be done" (Matthew 26:42).

Hearing this, Justice embraced and kissed Peace (Psalm 85:10), who had been standing at a distance, fearful because she did not know what the outcome would be. And so peace was achieved for those who were near and for those who were far away in one man, Christ, the mediator (Ephesians 2:17). For Christ is the truth rising from the earth—that is, from blessed Mary. He is the justice of the Father from heaven (Psalm 85:11)—that is, from the highest reaches of his judgment.

On earth he watched out for humanity and took care that anyone who could not be saved except in a just fashion, was justly saved. The truth has risen from the earth. The Lord bestowed his kindness (Psalm 85:12), namely the grace of the Holy Spirit. Our earth, that is the body of our Virgin, has given forth its fruit (Psalm 85:12). Justice will walk before him (Psalm 85:13), who is that fruit, and he will, as a result, place his feet onto the road of human salvation so that, as we have said, the human race, which could not be saved except in a just fashion, may be justly saved. ∾

The Parables and The Sentences

OUT OF BETHLEHEM

J*esus Christ, the Son of God, is born in Bethlehem-Judah* (Matthew 2:1). O what a little word this is about the Word made little! How marvelous is this holy birth transcending nature, yet for nature's sake! Why was the Son of God made man, except that we might be made the sons of God? The Son of God desired to have brothers, that he might be the First-born among many (Romans 8:29).

"Jesus Christ is born in Bethlehem-Judah." What condescension! Not in Jerusalem, the royal city, but in little Bethlehem. And Bethlehem of *Judah*, which reminds us of the promise given to his ancestors, "The scepter shall not depart from Judah, nor a leader from his loins, until he comes who shall be sent; and on him shall the nations hope" (Genesis 49:10).

"Bethlehem" means House-of-Bread, and "Judah" means Confession. Fill your soul with the food of the Word of God, and faithfully and with all possible devotion (though you can never offer such as it deserves), receive that Bread that comes down from heaven and gives life to the world (John 6:33). Live by faith (Hebrews 10:38). Then you yourself become a Bethlehem, and worthy to receive the Lord, provided that confession is not lacking. For, as the Apostle says, "Man believes with his heart and so is made righteous, and he confesses with his lips and so is saved" (Romans 10:9). Righteousness is as bread in the house, for righteousness is bread, so blessed are they that hunger and thirst for it (Matthew 5:6). Have, therefore, in your heart the righteousness that is of faith (Romans 10:6), and in your mouth confession that leads to salvation (10:9). Then you will receive with confidence him who is born in Bethlehem-Judah, Jesus Christ, the Son of God. ❧

Sermon on the Vigil of the Birth of the Lord

BLESSED ARE THE MERCIFUL

For him who prays for mercy, there is a fitting reply. "Blessed are the merciful, for they shall obtain mercy" (Matthew 5:7). Have mercy on your own soul (Sirach 30:24) if you want God to have mercy on you. Drench your bed in tears night after night, and remember to water your couch with weeping (Psalm 6:6). If you take compassion on yourself, if you labor with groans of repentance (Psalm 6:7)—for this is your first step in mercy— you will indeed find mercy. If you are perhaps a great sinner with many sins, and you ask a great mercy and many acts of pity (Psalm 51:2), you, too, must strive to show mercy. Be reconciled to yourself, for you did yourself grave injury (Job 7:20) in setting yourself up against God.

Now that peace has been restored in your own house, it is necessary first to extend it to your neighbor, and that he may give you a new kiss with the kiss of his mouth (Song of Songs 1:2); as it is written, you must be reconciled and at peace with God (Romans 5:1). Forgive those who have sinned against you, and your own sins will be forgiven you

(Luke 6:37); and you will pray to the Father with a quiet conscience, and say, "Forgive us our sins as we forgive those who sin against us" (Matthew 6:12).

If perhaps you have cheated anyone, make good what you owe, and give what is left over to the poor (Luke 19:8; 18:22; 11:41), and you will be shown mercy (Romans 9:25). "If your sins were scarlet, they shall be as white as snow, and if they were red as vermilion, they shall be white as wool" (Isaiah 1:18). So that you may not be put to shame for all the devices of your wrongdoing (Wisdom 3:11), for which you blush now (Romans 6:21), give alms, and if you cannot do so from your earthly substance (Luke 11:41), do it from your good will, and they will all be clean. Not only will the reason be enlightened and the will put right, but the memory itself will be purged, and you will cry to the Lord and hear a voice saying, "Blessed are the pure in heart, for they shall see God" (Matthew 5:8).

Chapter Sixteen
On Conversion

The End of Sorrow

I myself, however wretched I may be, have been occasionally privileged to sit at the feet of the Lord Jesus (Luke 10:39), and as much as that his merciful love allowed, I have embraced with all my heart, now one, now the other of these feet. And if, as happened at times, I should grow forgetful of his mercy, and with a tortured conscience become too deeply involved in the thought of the judgment, sooner or later I was cast down in unbelievable fear and shameful misery. Enveloped in a frightful gloom, I cried in dismay: "Who has yet felt the full force of your fury, or learnt to fear the violence of your rage?" (Psalm 90:11). But if on escaping from this I should cling more than was becoming to the foot of mercy, the opposite happened. I became worn, indifferent, negligent, lukewarm at prayer, listless at work, always on the watch for a laugh, inclined to say the wrong thing. And my interior was no steadier than my behavior.

But you know what a teacher experience is. No longer of judgment alone or mercy alone, but of mercy and judgment I will sing to you, O Lord (Psalm 101:1)!

I shall never forget your precepts (Psalm 119:93). Mercy and judgment will be the theme of my songs in the house of my pilgrimage (Psalm 119:54), until one day when mercy triumphs over judgment (James 2:13), my wretchedness will cease to sting, and my heart, silent no longer, will sing to you (Psalm 30:12). It will be the end of sorrow. ❧

Sermon Six
On the Song of Songs I

Healing the Wounds of Sin

Just as a doctor comes to a wounded man, so the Holy Spirit comes to the soul. Is it possible to find any person whom the devil's sword does not wound, even after the wound of original sin has been healed by the medicine of baptism? Therefore, when the Spirit draws near to a soul that says: "My wounds grow foul and fester because of my foolishness" (Psalm 38:5), what is the first thing he should do? Before all else he must amputate the ulcerous tumor that has grown upon the wound and prevents its healing.

This ulcer, caused by deep-rooted bad habits, must be sliced away with the scalpel of piercing sorrow. The pain will be bitter, but it can be alleviated with the ointment of devotion, which is nothing other than the joy born of the hope of pardon. This in turn springs from the power of self-control, from victory over sin. Soon the victor is pouring out words of thanksgiving: "You have loosed my bonds, I will offer you the thanksgiving sacrifice" (Psalm 116:16-17).

He then applies the medicine of penance, a dressing of fastings, vigils, prayers, and other tasks that penitents perform. And as he toils he must be fed with the food of good works so that he may not falter. We are not left in doubt about what the necessary food is: "My food," said Christ, "is to do the will of my Father" (John 4:34). Thus works motivated by love, that are a sure source of strength, should accompany the performance of penance. For instance it is said: "Alms is a most effective offering for all those who give it in the presence of the Most High" (Tobit 4:11).

Food causes thirst, therefore one must drink, so let the food of good works be moistened with the beverage of prayer, that a work well done may rest quietly in the stomach of conscience and give pleasure to God. In prayer one drinks the wine that gladdens a man's heart (Psalm 104:15), the intoxicating wine of the Spirit that drowns all memory of the pleasures of the flesh. It refreshes the arid recesses of the conscience, stimulates digestion of the meats of good works, fills the soul with a robust faith, a solid hope, a love that is living and true. It enriches all the actions of our life. ∽

Sermon Eighteen
On the Song of Songs I

4

Prayer

In Him Are All Things

Anyone who wishes to pray must choose not only the right place but also the right time. A time of leisure is best and most convenient. The deep silence when others are asleep is particularly suitable, for prayer will then be freer and purer.

You will not pray well, if in your prayers you seek anything but the Word, or seek him for the sake of anything but the Word, for in him are all things (Colossians 1:17). In him is healing for your wounds, help in your need, forgiveness for your faults, resources for your further growth. In him is all that anyone should ask or desire, all they need, all that will benefit them. There is no reason therefore to ask anything else of the Word, for he is all. Even if we seem sometimes to ask for material things—providing that we do so for the sake of the Word, as we should—it is not the things themselves that we are asking for, but him for whose sake we ask them. Those who habitually use all things to find the Word know this. ॐ

Sermon Eighty-six
On the Song of Songs IV

THE COMING OF THE WORD

I admit that the Word has come to me and has come many times. But although he has come to me, I have never been conscious of the moment of his coming. I perceived his presence, and I remembered afterwards that he had been with me; sometimes I had an inkling that he would come, but I was never conscious of his coming or his going. And where he comes from when he visits my soul, and where he goes, and how he enters and goes out, I admit that I do not know even now. As John says: "You do not know where he comes from nor where he goes" (John 3:8).

The coming of the Word was not perceptible to my eyes, for he has no color; nor to my ears, for there was no sound; nor yet to my nose, for he mingles with the mind, not the air. His coming was not tasted by the mouth, for there was no eating or drinking, nor could he be known by the sense of touch, for he is not tangible. How then did he enter?

Perhaps he did not enter because he does not come from outside? He is not one of the things which exist outside us. Yet he does not come from within me, for he is good, and I know that there is no good in me. I have searched the highest in me, and look! The Word is towering above that. In my curiosity I have explored my lowest depths, yet I found him even deeper. If I looked outside myself, I saw him stretching beyond the furthest I could see; and if I looked within, he was yet further within. Then I knew the truth of what I had read, "In him we live and move and have our being" (Acts 17:28).

So when the Bridegroom, the Word, came to me, he never made known his coming by any signs—not by sight, not by sound, not by touch. It was not by any movement of his that I recognized his coming. It was not by any of my senses that I perceived he had penetrated to the depths of my being. Only by the movement of my heart, as I have told you, did I perceive his presence. And I knew the power of his might (Ephesians 1:19) because my faults were put to flight and my human desires brought into subjection.

But when the Word has left me, all these spiritual powers become weak and faint and begin to grow cold, as though you had removed the fire from under a boiling pot. This is the sign of his going. Then my soul is sorrowful until he returns, and my heart again kindles within me—the sign of his returning. When I have had such experience of the Word, is it any wonder that I take to myself the words of the Bride, calling him back when he has withdrawn (Song of Songs 5:6)? For although my fervor is not as strong as hers, yet I am transported by a desire like hers. As long as I live, the word "return," the word of recall for the recall of the Word, will be on my lips.

As often as he slips away from me, so often shall I call him back. From the burning desire of my heart I will not cease to call him, begging him to return, as if after someone who is departing. I will implore him to give back to me the joy of his salvation, and restore himself to me (Psalm 51:12). ❧

Sermon Seventy-four
On the Song of Songs IV

THEY HAVE NO WINE

Learn from the great faith which the Lord's mother had in the wonders he could do. She preserved her modesty in great faith. Learn that modesty is the ornament of faith. . . . "They have no wine," she says (John 2:3). How briefly, how reverently she put the problem to him, despite her holy anxiety.

Learn, too, that in such circumstances it is much more holy to complain gently rather than to demand presumptuously, and better to give the shadowy expression of modesty to strong feeling and to speak quietly in prayer in the faith you have. She did not come up to him boldly. She did not speak to him openly and say frankly in everyone's hearing, "I beg you, son, the wine has run out, the guests grow solemn, the Bridegroom is embarrassed—show them what you can do."

Certainly her burning breast and aching heart would have said this or much more, but the holy Mother came to her powerful Son privately. She did not come to test his power but to see what his will might be. "They have no wine," she said. What could be more modest? What could be more trusting? Her faith was secure, her voice low; her desire prevailed. ❧

Chapter Twenty-two
On the Steps of Humility and Pride

Gather Up the Fragments with Gratitude

Learn not to be slow or sluggish in offering thanks. Learn to offer thanks for each and every gift. Take careful note, Scripture advises, of what is set before you (Proverbs 23:1), so that no gift of God, be it great or mediocre or small, will be deprived of due thanksgiving. We are even commanded to gather up the fragments, lest they be lost (John 6:12), which means that we are not to forget even the smallest benefits. What is given to an ungrateful person is surely lost. Ingratitude is our enemy—canceling our good deeds, weakening our virtues, wasting our benefits. Ingratitude is a burning wind that dries up the source of love, the dew of mercy, the streams of grace. ॐ

Sermon Fifty-one
On the Song of Songs III

SWEETER THAN HONEY

As food is sweet to the palate, so does a psalm delight the heart. But those who are sincere and wise will not fail to "chew" the psalm with their mind. If they "swallow" it in a lump, without properly chewing, the palate will be cheated of the delicious flavor, sweeter even than honey that drips from the comb (Psalm 19:10).

Let us with the apostles offer a honeycomb at the table of the Lord in the heavenly banquet. As honey flows from the comb, so should devotion flow from the words. Otherwise, if one attempts to digest them without the seasonings of the Spirit, "the written letters bring death" (2 Corinthians 3:6). But if like St. Paul, you sing praises not only with the spirit but with the mind as well (1 Corinthians 14:15), you too will experience the truth of Jesus' statement: "The words I have spoken to you are spirit, and they are life" (John 6:63). You will discover, too, the truths of the words of Wisdom: "The remembrance of me is sweeter than honey" (Sirach 24:20).

Sermon Seven
On the Song of Songs I

THE BRIDEGROOM IS PRESENT

Our meditations on the Word who is the Bridegroom, on his glory, his elegance, power and majesty, become in a sense his way of speaking to us. And not only that, but when with eager minds we examine his rulings, the decrees from his own mouth (Psalm 119:13), when we meditate on his law day and night (Psalm 1:2), let us be assured that the Bridegroom is present. He speaks his message of happiness to us so that our trials will not prove to be more than we can bear. ∞

Sermon Thirty-two
On the Song of Songs II

THANKSGIVING SACRIFICE

The sacrifice of our thanksgiving (Psalm 50:14) which we offer up should be threefold. It should be heartfelt, so that our mind is one with our words. It should bear fruit, so as to build up anyone who witnesses it. And it should be gracious, in order to be pleasing to the Creator who has himself given so freely. ❧

The Parables and The Sentences

WISE COUNSEL FOR PRAYER

Seven characteristics are required in prayers. Prayer should be faithful, in accordance with the Scripture: "Whatever you pray for, believe that you already have it, and it will be yours" (Mark 11:24). Then prayer should be pure, after the example of Abraham, who drove the birds away from his sacrifice (Genesis 15:11). Third, it should be just. Fourth, it should be heartfelt, since "the heartfelt prayer of a just person works very powerfully" (James 5:16). Fifth, it should be humble; sixth, it should be fervent (these last two characteristics you see in the mustard seed). And seventh, it should be devout. ❧

The Parables and The Sentences

Rapt in God

The first and greatest kind of contemplation is to wonder at majesty. This demands a heart made pure, so that, freed from vices and released from sin, it can ascend easily to heavenly things. Sometimes this contemplation holds the watcher rapt in amazement and ecstasy, if only for a moment.

A second kind of contemplation is necessary for this man. He needs to look on the judgments of God. While this contemplation strikes fear into the onlooker because it is indeed frightening, it drives out vices, strengthens virtues, initiates into wisdom, protects humility. Humility is the true and solid foundation of the virtues. For if humility were to collapse, the building-up of the virtues would fall down.

The third kind of contemplation is occupied (or rather at leisure) in remembering kindnesses and, so as to avoid ingratitude, it urges him who remembers to love his Benefactor. Of such says the Prophet, speaking to the Lord, "They shall declare the memory of the abundance of your sweetness" (Psalm 145:7).

The fourth contemplation, which forgets what is past, rests wholly in the expectation of what is promised (Philippians 3:13), which nourishes patience and nerves the arm of perseverance, for what is promised is eternal. ❧

Chapter Fourteen
On Consideration

Increasing the Grace of Devotion

Four things are said to increase the grace of our devotion: the recollection of our sins, which makes a person humble; the remembrance of punishment, which encourages him to act well; the consideration of his pilgrimage on this earth, which urges him to spurn visible goods; and the desire for everlasting life, which encourages him toward perfection and impels him to withdraw from worldly attachments by a change in his will. ❧

The Parables and The Sentences

5

Pure of Heart

ALL IN ALL

Since Scripture says God made everything for his own purpose (Proverbs 16:4), the day must come when all creation will conform to and agree with its Maker. It is therefore necessary for us to reach a similar state in which, just as God willed everything to exist for himself, so we wish that we ourselves and everyone else live only for his will alone, and not for our own pleasure. The satisfaction of our wants, chance happiness, delights us less than to see his will done in us and for us, which we implore every day in prayer, saying: "Your will be done on earth as it is in heaven" (Matthew 6:10).

O pure and holy love! O sweet and pleasant affection! O pure and sinless intention of the will, all the more sinless and pure since it frees us from the taint of selfish vanity, all the more sweet and pleasant, for all that is found in it is divine. To reach this state is to become like God. As a drop of water seems to disappear completely in a big quantity of wine, even assuming the wine's taste and color; just as red, molten iron becomes so much like fire it seems to lose its primary state; just as the air on a sunny day seems transformed into sunshine instead of being lit up; so it is necessary for the saints that all human feelings melt in a mysterious way and flow into the will of God. Otherwise, how will God be all in all (1 Corinthians 15:28) if something human survives in man? ❧

Chapter Ten
On Loving God

THE YOKE OF CHRIST

For my yoke is easy and my burden light (Matthew 11:30). There is a burden which carries the one who lifts it up and makes him light. It is that light burden of the gospel, that yoke of Christ which is easy for those who have turned to him. For one who previously had been unable to shoulder the commands of the law, afterward finds the precepts of the gospel light with the assistance of grace. A person who had previously been unable to fulfill the commandment not to kill (Exodus 20:13) later finds it easy to lay down his life for others (1 John 3:16).

It is the same with the other commandments. Thus, when a weighty load is forced upon a beast of burden and he flees from it as though it were impossible to carry, a swift wagon is brought forward—that is, the gospel, which rushes through the whole world—and the burden which the beast first refused as being too heavy it afterward pulls easily, even if it is doubled. It is the same with a little bird. Unfledged and wingless, it cannot lift itself in flight, but when the weight of feathers and wings is added, it easily soars. Think too of hard bread. By itself it cannot be swallowed, but when milk or some other liquid is added to it, it becomes perfectly possible for it to glide down the throat. ❧

The Parables and The Sentences

WITHOUT STAIN OR WRINKLE

Blessed are the pure in heart, for they shall see God (Matthew 5:8). This is a great promise and something to be desired with all one's heart. For to see in this way is to be like God, as John the Apostle says: "Now we are all sons of God, but it has not yet been made clear what we shall be. For we know that when it is made clear we shall be like him, for we shall see him as he is" (1 John 3:2). This vision is eternal life (John 12:50), as Truth himself says in the Gospel, "This is eternal life, that they should know that you alone are the true God, and him whom you have sent, Jesus Christ" (17:3).

Hateful is the blemish which deprives us of this blessed vision. Detestable is the neglect which causes us to put off the cleansing of the eye. For just as our bodily vision is impeded either by fluid within or by dust outside entering the eye, so too is our spiritual vision disturbed by the desires of our own flesh or by worldly curiosity and ambition. Our own experience teaches us this, no less than the Sacred Page, where it is written, "The body which is corruptible weighs down the soul and the earthly habitation oppresses its thoughts" (Wisdom 9:15). But in both it is sin alone which dulls and confuses the vision. Nothing else seems to stand between the eye and the light, between God and man. For while we are in this body we are in exile from the Lord (2 Corinthians 5:6).

That is not the body's fault, except in that it is yet mortal (Romans 7:24). Rather, it is the flesh which is a sinful body (6:6), the flesh in which there is no good thing but rather where the law of sin reigns (7:23,25). Meanwhile the bodily eye, when the mote is no longer in it but has been taken or blown away, still seems dark, as he who walks in the Spirit and sees deeply often experiences (2 Corinthians 12:18; Galatians 5:16). For you will cure a wounded limb quickly by withdrawing the sword, but only if you apply poultices to heal it. For no one should think himself cleansed because he has come out of the cesspit. No, rather let him realize that he stands in need of a thorough washing first. Nor must he be washed only with water; he needs to be purged and refined by fire so as to say, "We have passed through fire and water, and you have brought us to a resting place" (Psalm 66:12).

"Blessed are the pure in heart, for they shall see God" (Matthew 5:8). "Now we see through a glass darkly, but hereafter face to face" (1 Corinthians 13:12). Then truly our faces will be completely clean, so that he may present them to himself shining, without stain or wrinkle (Ephesians 5:27). ❧

Chapter Seventeen
On Conversion

THE FOLLIES OF PRIDE

One sort of pride is blind, a second is vain, and a third both blind and vain. Pride is blind when a person thinks there is in him what is not there. It is vain when he glories in the fact that people take him to be what he is not. And it is both blind and vain when he glories inwardly and seeks the respect of others for having a good which he does not possess. ❧

The Parables and The Sentences

LEANING ON GOD

Who shall ascend the hill of the Lord? (Psalm 24:3). If anyone longs to climb to the summit of that mountain—to the perfection of virtue—he will know how hard the climb is. Any attempt is doomed to failure without the help of the Word. Happy are they who cause the angels to look at them with joy and wonder and hear them saying, "Who is this coming up from the wilderness, rich in grace and beauty, leaning upon her beloved?" (Song of Songs 8:5). Otherwise, unless they lean on God, they struggle in vain. But they will gain force by struggling with themselves and, becoming stronger, will impel all things towards reason: anger, fear, covetousness, and joy.

Surely all things are possible to someone who leans on God who can do all things? What confidence there is in the cry, "I can do all things in him who strengthens me!" (Philippians 4:13). Nothing shows more clearly the almighty power of the Word than that he makes all-powerful all those who put their hope in him. For "all things are possible to one who believes" (Mark 9:23). If all things are possible to him, he must be all-powerful. Thus, if they do not rely upon themselves, but are strengthened by the Word, they can gain such command over themselves that nothing unrighteous will have power over them. So, I say, neither power, nor treachery, nor temptation, can overthrow or hold in subjection those whose minds rest upon the Word and are clothed with strength from above (Luke 24:49).

Sermon Eighty-five
On the Song of Songs IV

The Way, the Truth, and the Life

I *am the way, the truth, and the life* (John 14:6). The way, our Lord says, is humility, which leads to truth. The first is labor; the second is the reward for the labor (1 Corinthians 3:8). But, you ask, how do I know that he is speaking of humility when he says only, "I am the way"? Listen to this clearer statement, "Learn from me, for I am meek and humble of heart" (Matthew 11:29). He offers himself as an example of humility, a model of gentleness. If you imitate him you will not walk in darkness; you will have the light of life (John 8:12). What is the light of life but truth, which enlightens every man who comes into this world (1:9), showing him where true life lies (1 Timothy 6:19)? That is why when he said, "I am the way, the truth," he added, "and the life," which, he says, "I give." "For this is eternal life," he says, "to know that you are the true God and to know him whom you have sent, Jesus Christ" (John 17:3). Or it is as though you were to say, "I reflect on the way; that is humility. I desire the reward, which is truth. But what if the way is so difficult that I cannot reach the desired reward?" He replies, "I am the life," that is, food for the journey (Deuteronomy 15:14; Joshua 9:5).

To those who go astray and do not know the road, he says, "I am the way." To those who hesitate to believe, he says, "I am the truth." To those who are already climbing, he says, "I am the life." ༄

Chapter One
On the Steps of Humility and Pride

CHOOSE THE LAST PLACE

Just as the fear of the Lord is the beginning of all wisdom (Psalm 111:10; Sirach 1:16), so pride is the beginning of all sin (Sirach 10:13). Just as love of God is the way to the perfection of wisdom, so despair leads to the committing of every sin. And so the fear of God springs up within you from knowledge of self and the love of God from the knowledge of God. On the other hand, pride comes from lack of self-knowledge and despair from lack of knowledge of God. Ignorance of what you are contributes to your pride, because your deluded and deluding thoughts lie to you, telling you that you are better than you are. For this is pride, this is how all sin originates—that you are greater in your own eyes than you are before God, than you are in truth.

There is no risk involved then, no matter how much you lower yourself, no matter how much your self-esteem falls short of what you are—that is, of what Truth thinks of you. But the evil is great and the risk frightening if you exult yourself even a little above what you are, or if in your thoughts you consider yourself of more worth than even one person whom Truth may judge your equal or your better.

To make myself clearer: If you pass through a low doorway you suffer no hurt, however much you bend. But if you raise your head higher than the doorway, even by a finger's breadth, you will dash it against the lintel and injure yourself. So also a man has no need to fear any humiliation, but he should quake with fear before rashly exalting himself even a little. So then, beware of comparing yourself with your betters or your inferiors, with a particular few or with even one. Perhaps you regard this one person as the vilest and most wretched of all, whose life you recoil from and spurn as more offensive and wicked, not merely than yours—for you trust you are a sober-living man and just and religious—but even than all other wicked men. How do you know, I say, that in time to come, with the aid of the right hand of the Most High (Psalm 77:10), he will not surpass both you and them if he has not done so already in God's sight?

That is why God wished us to choose neither a middle seat nor the second to the last one, nor even one of the lowest rank. He said, "Sit down in the lowest place" (Luke 14:10), that you may sit alone, last of all, and not dare to compare yourself, still less to prefer yourself, to anyone. See how great the evil that springs from our lack of self-knowledge—nothing less than the devil's sin and the beginning of every sin, pride (Sirach 10:13). ∽

Sermon Thirty-seven
On the Song of Songs II

GOLIATH AND THE VICE OF PRIDE

Elated and inflated by the spirit of his flesh, Goliath alone dared to insult the people of God (1 Samuel 17:8-9) who had already entered the promised land and triumphed over many enemies! I believe that this proud man might appropriately represent the vice of pride. Pride is the greatest sin, because it taunts the people of God to a higher degree, and especially rises up against those who seem to have already conquered the other sins. Therefore, once the others have been subdued, pride challenges to single combat.

At that time, the Philistines were altogether

afraid to engage in battle against Israel, except only that all their confidence hung on Goliath, a man of enormous size. Now, for what reason would pride tempt a soul of that kind? How, I say, would pride dominate someone when other vices such as envy, lukewarmness or laziness already dominate so much? Finally, who but a strong-handed man (Joshua 1:14), one who has already subdued the remaining vices by his powerful strength, would come forward to contend against the perfectly vile vice of pride? Let David go forward, I say, strong-handed, because such a great enemy is not conquered except by a strong hand (Exodus 13:3). Let the one who has conquered the bear and the lion (1 Samuel 17:34-35) arm himself against Goliath!

And so, having rejected Saul's arms, David picked up five stones from the stream (1 Samuel 17:40). . . . These five stones can be understood as the five kinds of words: of warning, promise, love, imitation, and prayer. Of course an abundance of these words is found everywhere accessible in the Scriptures.

Now surely David, as he is about to contend with the spirit of pride, is storing those five stones he picked up in the pouch, which is his memory. He considers how great are God's warnings to us, how much he promises, how great a love he shows us, how many examples of holiness he offers, and, finally, how he urges us everywhere to earnestness in prayer. Let anyone who is hastening to vanquish the vice of pride bear these stones with him. Then, I say, as often as the venomous head dares to rise, and whichever of these stones first presents itself to the hand of his thought, Goliath may be struck on the forehead, cast down, and covered with shame (1 Samuel 17:49). A sling, in the shape of long-suffering, is also clearly necessary in this conflict. For no reason can it be absent from this combat.

Whenever the thought of vainglory agitates your mind, if from your heart's deepest inclination you begin to fear God's warnings or to long for his promises, Goliath will not withstand the blow of either of these stones. Every swelling will be immediately checked. If such an indescribable love as God's majesty has shown you comes into your mind, do you not immediately, as you take fire with this love, begin right away to detest and abandon vainglory? Thus, too, if you put the examples given by the saints before you for your careful consideration, this will undoubtedly serve to check your self-exaltation. Moreover if perhaps, as self-exaltation suddenly arises, your hand cannot take hold of any of these stones we have mentioned, turn with all fervor toward what alone remains—prayer. Immediately this ungodly one whom you had seen elevated and exalted like the cedars of Lebanon, having been overthrown, will be no more (Psalm 37:35-36).

But perhaps you are asking how you may be able to cut off Goliath's head with his own sword (1 Samuel 17:51)? That would be the more agreeable to you as it would be more grievous to the enemy. I shall be brief since I speak to the experienced, and they grasp easily and remark without delay what they perceive repeatedly acted out within themselves. As often as, at vainglory's challenge, you begin to be ashamed and to blush when you remember God's warnings, or promise, or the other stones we spoke of, Goliath has indeed been cast down, but is perhaps still living. So come up closer, in case he rises up again. Standing over him, cut off his head with his own sword's point, destroying vainglory with the very vainglory that assails you. You have slain Goliath with the sword of Goliath if, struck by that haughty thought, you take from it the material and occasion for humility. Regard yourself from now on as humbly and lowly as you regard that proud man.

Sermon on the Fourth Sunday after Pentecost

THE SCALE OF KNOWLEDGE

Knowledge for its own sake is curiosity. Knowledge which exists in order to be seen is vanity. Knowledge which exists in order to help one's brother or sister is charity. Knowledge which aims at loving God and molding one's life is wisdom. This kind of knowledge is embraced, however, not with the help of writing or memory, but by the disposition of a devout mind and through a good conscience.

The Parables and The Sentences

THE LORD HAS NEED OF THESE

Within us we have a castle which is opposed to us—that is, our own will, whose wall is obstinacy, whose tower is pride, whose weapons are our wicked excuses, and whose supplies are our perverse pleasures.

In this castle the ass—that is, obedience—is tied up, along with her colt, which is humility (Matthew 21:2). They are tied with the chains of sin, about which it is written, "The ropes of sin have tightened around me" (Psalm 119:61).

Christ sends to the castle two of his disciples, mercy and truth. Thus it is written: "Mercy and truth go before you" (Psalm 89:14). Mercy loosens the chains, while truth draws the animals out and leads them to the confession of sin, which is signified by Jesus as he entered Jerusalem. "Untie them," Christ says, "and bring them to me" (Matthew 21:2).

Mercy frees, and truth directs. So it is said: "Belief in the heart leads to justice, and confession of tongue brings about salvation" (Romans 10:10). Still further, "The word in your mouth is near" for confession "and in your heart for believing" (10:8).

There are some who are accustomed to defending their actions, because their own ways seem right to them, rather than the instruction of their superiors. But it is written to the contrary: "The Lord has need of these" (Matthew 21:3), namely of obedience and humility, rather than of those things which arise from one's own will. To explain it another way, the ass represents simplicity, and the colt humility.

When it is said that "The Lord has need of these," it means that anyone who desires to be governed rightly by others has need of simplicity as opposed to cleverness, and of humility as opposed to pride. ∾

The Parables and The Sentences

THE THREE GRADES OF OBEDIENCE

There are three grades of obedience. When one is anxious that he may transgress, he exhibits an obedience which derives from fear. Then, when one obeys out of a hope for reward, he exhibits an obedience which aims to be praiseworthy. Finally there is pure and loving obedience, exhibited by one who trusts that all the things that belong to his Father are also his (John 17:10). ∽

The Parables and The Sentences

6

Mary, Blessed Among Women

ALL CREATION AWAITS
MARY'S REPLY

Virgin, you have heard that you will conceive
and bear a son (Luke 1:31); you have heard that it
will be by the Holy Spirit and not by a man (1:35).
The angel is waiting for your reply. It is time for
him to return to the One who sent him. We, too,
are waiting for this merciful word, my lady, we who
are miserably weighed down under a sentence of
condemnation.

The price of our salvation is being offered you. If
you consent, we shall immediately be set free. We
all have been made in the eternal Word of God,
and look, we are dying (2 Corinthians 6:9). In your
brief reply we shall be restored and so brought back
to life.

Sorrowful Adam and his unhappy offspring, exiled from Paradise, implore you, kind Virgin, to give this answer. David asks it. Abraham asks it. All the other holy patriarchs, your very own fathers beg it of you, as do those now dwelling in the region of the shadow of death (Isaiah 9:2). For it the whole world is waiting, bowed down at your feet. And rightly so, because on your answer depends the comfort of the afflicted; the redemption of captives; the deliverance of the damned; the salvation of all the sons of Adam, your whole race.

So, answer the angel quickly or rather, through the angel, answer God. Only say the word and receive the Word. Give yours and conceive God's. Breathe one fleeting word and embrace the ever-lasting Word.

Why do you delay? Why be afraid? Believe, give praise, and receive. Let humility take courage and shyness confidence. This is not the moment for virginal simplicity to forget prudence. In this circumstance, alone, O prudent Virgin, do not fear presumptuousness, for if your reserve pleased by its silence, now much more must your goodness speak. Blessed Virgin, open your heart to faith, your lips to consent, and your womb to your Creator. Behold, the long-desired of all nations is standing at the door and knocking (Revelation 3:20). Oh, what if he should pass by because of your delay and, sorrowing, you should again have to seek him whom your soul loves (Song of Songs 3:1-4)? Get up, run, open! Get up by faith, run by prayer, open by consent!

"Behold," she says, "I am the handmaiden of the Lord; let it be to me according to your word" (Luke 1:38). ◈

Homily Four
In Praise of the Virgin Mother

RESTORED TO LIFE THROUGH THE DAUGHTER OF EVE

Rejoice, Adam, our father, and you more especially, mother Eve, exult. You were the parents of mankind and the destroyers of mankind and, most wretchedly, our destroyers even before you were our parents. Now let both of you, I say, take consolation in your daughter and in so great a daughter, especially you, Eve, whose reproach has been handed down to all womankind.

The time has now come for your reproach to be taken away. No longer will man have any reason to accuse woman as he did long ago when, attempting cowardly to excuse himself, he did not hesitate cruelly to accuse her, saying, "The woman whom you gave to be with me, she gave me the fruit of the tree and I ate it" (Genesis 3:12).

Eve, run then to Mary, run to your daughter. Let your daughter now plead for her mother and take away her mother's reproach. Let her now reconcile her mother to the Father. For if man fell on account of woman, surely he will rise only through another woman.

What was it you said, Adam? "The woman whom you gave to be with me, she gave me the fruit of the tree, and I ate" (Genesis 3:12). What evil words! Far from excusing you, they condemn you (Wisdom 17:11). However, Wisdom prevails against evil (7:30). The occasion for pardon which God endeavored to draw from you by his cross-examination but could not, he found in the treasure of his never-failing kindness. Yes, he gave woman for woman: a wise one for a foolish one; a humble one for an arrogant one. Instead of the tree of death, she offers you a taste of life. In place of the poisonous fruit of bitterness, she holds out to you the sweetness of eternity's fruit.

Change your words of evil excuse into a song of thanksgiving then and say, "Lord, the woman whom you gave to be with me, she gave me the fruit of the tree of life, and I ate; and it was sweeter than honey to my mouth (Genesis 3:12; Psalm 119:103), for by it have you given me life."

Behold, for this was the angel sent to a virgin. O Virgin maid, admirable and worthy of all our honor (Song of Songs 7:6). O uniquely venerable woman! O fairest among all women! You have repaired your parents' weakness, and restored life to all their offspring.

Homily Two
In Praise of the Virgin Mother

LET US IMITATE MARY

The angel Gabriel was sent by God (Luke 1:26). To whom? "To a virgin engaged to a man whose name was Joseph" (1:27). Who is this virgin noble enough to be greeted by an angel and yet humble enough to be the fiancé of a workman?

How gracious is this union of virginity and humility! A soul in whom humility embellishes virginity and virginity ennobles humility finds no little favor with God. Imagine then how much more worthy of reverence must she have been whose humility was raised by motherhood and whose virginity consecrated by her childbearing. You are told that she is a virgin. You are told that she is humble. If you are not able to imitate the virginity of this humble maid, then imitate the humility of the virgin maid.

Virginity is a praiseworthy virtue, but humility is by far the more necessary. The one is only counseled; the other is demanded. To the first you have been invited; to the second you are obligated. Concerning the first Jesus said, "He who is able to receive this, let him receive it" (Matthew 19:12). Of the second he said, "Truly I said to you, unless you become like this little child, you will not enter the kingdom of heaven" (18:3). The first is rewarded; the second is required. You can be saved without virginity; without humility you cannot be. Humility which regrets the loss of virginity can still find favor. Yet I dare to say that without humility not even Mary's virginity would have been acceptable.

The Lord says, "Upon whom shall my Spirit rest, if not upon him that is humble and contrite in spirit?" (Isaiah 66:2). *On the humble,* he says, not on the virgin. Had Mary not been humble, then the Holy Spirit would not have rested upon her. Had he not rested upon her, she would not have become pregnant. How indeed could she have conceived by him without him? It seems evident then that she conceived by the Holy Spirit (Luke 1:35) because, as she herself said, God "regarded the humility of his handmaiden" (1:48) rather than her virginity. And even if it was because of her virginity that she found favor, she conceived nevertheless on account of her humility. Thus there is no doubt that her virginity was found pleasing because her humility made it so. ❧

Homily One
In Praise of the Virgin Mother

Unparalleled Wonder

Never since the world began has it been known for any woman to be at once a mother and a virgin. If you think whose mother Mary is, surely you must be astounded at such marvelous greatness. Who could ever admire this enough?

To your way of thinking, or rather, not yours but Truth's, should she not be exalted above all the choirs of angels, she who bore God the Son? Who else would dare, as Mary did, to call "son" the Lord and God of angels and to say, "Son, why have you treated us so?" (Luke 2:48). Would any angel dare this?

Yet Jesus was the same Majesty whom the angels serve with awe and reverence that Mary, knowing herself the mother, confidently called her son. Nor did God reject being called what he had agreed to become. As the Evangelist tells us a bit later, "He was obedient to them" (Luke 2:51). Who? God. To whom? To men. God, I repeat, to whom the angels are subject, he whom the principalities and the powers obey, he was obedient to Mary. And not only to Mary but to Joseph, too, for Mary's sake.

Marvel then at these two things: the gracious kindness of the Son and the surpassing dignity of the mother. Choose which you consider more wonderful. Just imagine! Double marvel! God does what a woman says—unheard of humility. A woman outranks God—unparalleled wonder. In praise of the virgins we sing that "they follow the Lamb wherever he goes" (Revelation 14:4). Of what praise then do you consider her worthy, who preceded him? ❧

Homily One
In Praise of the Virgin Mother

CALL OUT TO MARY

The virgin's name was Mary (Luke 1:27). Let us now say a few words about this name, which means "star of the sea" and is so becoming to the Virgin Mother. Surely she is very fittingly likened to a star.

The star sends forth its ray without harm to itself. In the same way the Virgin brought forth her son with no injury to herself. The ray no more diminishes the star's brightness than does the Son his mother's integrity. She is indeed that noble star risen out of Jacob (Numbers 24:17) whose beam enlightens this earthly globe. She it is whose brightness both twinkles in the highest heaven and pierces the pit of hell, and is shed upon earth, warming our hearts far more than our bodies, fostering virtue and burning out vice. She, I tell you, is that splendid and wondrous star suspended as by necessity over this great wide sea, radiant with goodness and brilliant in example.

O you, whoever you are, who feel that in the tidal wave of this world you are nearer to being tossed about among the squalls and gales than treading on dry land, if you do not want to founder in the tempest, do not avert your eyes from the brightness of this star. When the wind of temptation blows up within you, when you strike upon the rock of tribulation, gaze up at this star, call out to Mary. Whether you are being tossed about by the waves of pride or ambition or slander or jealousy, gaze up at this star, call out to Mary. When rage or greed or fleshly desires are battering the skiff of your soul, gaze up at Mary. When the immensity of your sins weighs you down and you are bewildered by the offensiveness of your conscience, when the terrifying thought of judgment appalls you and you begin to founder in the gulf of sadness and despair, think of Mary. In dangers, in hardships, in every doubt, think of Mary, call out to Mary.

Keep her in your mouth, keep her in your heart. Follow the example of her life and you will obtain the favor of her prayer. Following her, you will never go astray. Asking her help, you will never wander away. With your hand in hers, you will never stumble. With her protecting you, you will not be afraid. With her leading you, you will never tire. Her kindness will see you through to the end. Then you will know by your own experience how true it is that "the virgin's name was Mary" (Luke 1:27).

Homily Two
In Praise of the Virgin Mother

7

Desiring God Alone

JOY FULFILLED

It is a great good to seek God; in my opinion the soul knows no greater blessing. To seek God is the first gift of the soul and the final stage of its journey. Nothing is inferior to this, and nothing else yields to it. What could be superior, when nothing else has a higher place? What could claim a higher place, when it is the consummation of all things? What virtue can be attributed to anyone who does not seek God? What boundary can be set for anyone who does seek him?

The Psalmist says: "Seek his face always" (Psalm 105:4). Nor, I think, will anyone cease to seek God even when he has found him.

It is not with steps of the feet that God is sought but with the heart's desire. When someone happily finds him, his desire is not quenched but kindled. Does the consummation of joy bring about the consuming of desire? Rather it is oil poured upon the flames. So it is. Joy will be fulfilled (Psalm 16:11), but there will be no end to desire, and therefore no end to the search. Think, if you can, of this eagerness to see God as not caused by his absence, for he is always present; and think of the desire for God as without fear of failure, for grace is abundantly present. ❧

Sermon Eighty-four
On the Song of Songs IV

CONTEMPLATING THE SUN OF JUSTICE

Neither sage nor saint nor prophet can or could ever see God as he is, while still in this mortal body. But whoever is found worthy will be able to do so when the body becomes immortal. Though God is seen here below, it is in the form that seems good to him, not as he is.

For example, take that mighty source of light—I speak of that sun which you see day after day. Yet, you do not see it as it is, but as it lights up the air, or a mountain, or a wall. Nor could you see even to this extent if the light of your body, the eye (Matthew 6:22)—because of its natural steadiness and clearness—did not bear some degree of likeness to that light in the heavens. Since all the other members of the body lack this likeness, they are incapable of seeing the light. Even the eye itself, when troubled, cannot approach the light, because it has lost that likeness.

And so when you are enlightened you can see even now the Sun of Justice (Malachi 4:2) that "enlightens every man who comes into this world" (John 1:9), according to the degree of the light he gives. By this light you are made somehow like him. But you cannot see him as he is, because you are not yet perfectly like him. That is why the Psalmist says: "Come to him and be enlightened, and our faces shall never be ashamed" (Psalm 34:5). That is very true, provided we are enlightened as much as we need, so that "with our unveiled faces contemplating the glory of God, all grow brighter and brighter as we are turned into the same image, as by the Spirit of the Lord" (2 Corinthians 3:18). ❧

Sermon Thirty-one
On the Song of Songs II

THE SPOUSE OF THE WORD

When you see a soul leaving everything and clinging to the Word with all her will and desire, living for the Word, ruling her life by the Word, conceiving by the Word what it will bring forth by him, so that she can say, "For me to live is Christ, and to die is gain" (Philippians 1:21), you know that the soul is the spouse and bride of the Word. The heart of the Bridegroom has faith in her (Proverbs 31:11), knowing her to be faithful, for she has rejected all things as rubbish to gain him (Philippians 3:8). ❧

Sermon Eighty-five
On the Song of Songs IV

WE CAN NEVER BE SEPARATED

Bernard wrote this letter to comfort Abbot Suger on his deathbed:

To his dear and intimate friend Suger, by the grace of God Abbot of St. Denis, Brother Bernard sends glory from within and grace from on high.

Fear not, man of God, to put off the earthy man which is holding you down to the earth, and which would bring you down even to the regions under the earth. It is this which troubles, burdens, and aggrieves you. But why trouble about your clothing of flesh, when you are about to put on the garb of immortality in heaven? It is ready for you, but it will not be given to you already clothed; it will clothe you, but not while you are still clothed in the flesh. Wait patiently, and be glad to be found naked and unclothed. God himself wishes man to be clothed, but not while he is still clothed in the flesh (2 Corinthians 5:2-4). The man of God will not return to God, until what he has of the earth has gone back to the earth (Genesis 3:19). These two, the man of God and the earthly man, are at variance one with the other, and there will be no peace for you until they are separated; and if there should be peace, it would not be the peace of God, nor would it be peace with God. You are not one of those who say: "Peace, when there is no peace" (Jeremiah 6:14; 8:11). The peace which passes all understanding (Philippians 4:7) is awaiting you, and the righteous are waiting for this peace to be given you, and the joy of the Lord awaits you.

And I, dear friend, am torn by the desire to see you, that I may receive a dying man's blessing. But no man can arrange his life as he wishes, and so I cannot dare to promise what I am not sure of being able to perform; yet I will try my best to do what I am not yet able to see my way to doing. Perhaps I shall come, perhaps I shall not. But whatever happens I, who have loved you from the first, shall love you without end. I say with all confidence that I can never lose one whom I have loved unto the end: one to whom my soul cleaves so firmly that it can never be separated, does not go away but only goes before. Be mindful of me when you come to where I shall follow you, so that I may be permitted soon to come after you and come to you. In the meantime be sure that I shall never lose the dear memory of you, although to my sorrow I lose your dear presence. Yet God can keep you with us in answer to our prayers; he can still preserve you for those who need you, of this there can be no doubt. ❧

The Letters of St. Bernard of Clairvaux

FIX YOUR ATTENTION ON THE WAYS OF GOD

My advice to you, my friends, is to turn aside occasionally from troubled and anxious pondering on the paths you may be treading. Travel on smoother ways where the gifts of God are serenely savored, so that the thought of him may give breathing space to you whose consciences are perplexed. I should like you to experience for yourselves the truth of the holy Prophet's words: "Make the Lord your joy and he will give you what your heart desires" (Psalm 37:4).

Sorrow for sin is indeed necessary, but it should not be an endless preoccupation. You must dwell also on the glad remembrance of God's loving-kindness. Otherwise sadness will harden the heart and lead it more deeply into despair. Let us mix honey with our absinthe, as it is more easily drunk when sweetened, and what bitterness it may still retain will be wholesome. You must fix your attention on the ways of God. See how he mitigates the bitterness of the heart that is crushed, how he wins back the cowardly soul from the abyss of despair, how he consoles the grief-stricken and strengthens the wavering with the sweet caress of his faithful promise.

The Prophet declares: "For my praise I will bridle you, lest you should perish" (Isaiah 48:9). By this he seems to say: "Lest you should be cast down by excessive sadness at the sight of your sins, and rush despairingly to destruction like an unbridled horse over a precipice, I shall rein you in, I shall curb you with my mercy and set you on your feet with my praises. Then you will breathe freely again in the enjoyment of my benefits, overwhelmed though you may be by evils of your own making, because you will find that my kindness is greater than your guilt."

You are told in the Book of Wisdom: "Think of the Lord with goodness, seek him in simplicity of heart" (Wisdom 1:1). You will all the more easily achieve this if you let your mind dwell frequently, even continually, on the memory of God's bountifulness. Otherwise, how will you fulfill St. Paul's advice: "In all things give thanks to God" (1 Thessalonians 5:18), if your hearts will have lost sight of those things for which thanks are due? ❧

Sermon Eleven
On the Song of Songs I

SEEKING HIM WHO FIRST SOUGHT US

I *sought him whom my soul loves* (Song of Songs 3:1)—this is what you are urged to do by the goodness of him who anticipates you who sought him, and loved you before you loved him (1 John 4:10). You would not seek him or love him unless you had first been sought and loved. Not only one blessing has been prepared for you beforehand but two:

being loved as well as being sought. For the love is the reason for the search, and the search is the fruit of the love, and its certain proof. You are loved, so that you may not suppose you are sought to be punished. You are sought, so that you may not complain you are loved in vain. Both these loving and manifest favors give you courage, and drive away your hesitation, persuading you to return, and stirring your affections. From this comes the zeal and ardor to seek him whom your soul loves (Song of Songs 3:1), because you cannot seek unless you are sought, and when you are sought you cannot but seek.

Since I love, I cannot doubt that I am loved, any more than I can doubt that I love. Nor can I fear to look on his face, since I have sensed his tenderness. In what have I known it? In this—not only has he sought me as I am, but he has shown me tenderness, and caused me to seek him with confidence. How can I not respond to him when he seeks me, since I respond to him in tenderness? How can he be angry with me for seeking him, when he overlooked the contempt I showed him? He will not drive away someone who seeks him. . . . How can I fail to be inspired to seek him, when I have experienced his mercy and been assured of his peace? ❧

Sermon Eighty-four
On the Song of Songs IV

Sources and Acknowledgments

The editor and publisher wish to express their gratitude
to Dr. E. Rozanne Elder, Editorial Director,
and Cistercian Publications, Kalamazoo, Michigan,
for permission to adapt translations of the following
Cistercian material:

Homilies in Praise of the Blessed Virgin Mary, by
Bernard of Clairvaux, Cistercian Fathers Series No.
18A. Translated by Marie-Bernard Said, O.S.B.
© 1979 by Cistercian Publications.

The Letters of St. Bernard of Clairvaux. Translated
by Bruno Scott James. First published in the
United States by Cistercian Publications, 1998.
© Burns and Oates, 1953, 1998.

On Loving God by Bernard of Clairvaux. Cistercian
Fathers Series No. 13B. Translated by Robert
Walton, O.S.B. © 1973 by Cistercian Publications.

On the Song of Songs I, by Bernard of Clairvaux, Cistercian Fathers Series No. 4. Translated by Kilian Walsh, O.C.S.O. © 1971 by Cistercian Publications.

On the Song of Songs II, by Bernard of Clairvaux, Cistercian Fathers Series No. 7. Translated by Kilian Walsh, O.C.S.O. © 1976 by Cistercian Publications.

On the Song of Songs III, by Bernard of Clairvaux, Cistercian Fathers Series No. 31. Translated by Kilian Walsh, O.C.S.O. and Irene M. Edmonds. © 1979 by Cistercian Publications.

On the Song of Songs IV, by Bernard of Clairvaux, Cistercian Fathers Series No. 40. Translated by Irene M. Edmonds. © 1980 by Cistercian Publications.

Saint Bernard on the Christian Year: Selections from His Sermons. Translated and edited by a Religious of CSMV. A. R. Mowbray & Co. Limited, London, 1954.

For Further Reading

Bernard of Clairvaux: Essential Writings, by Dennis
E. Tamburello, O.F.M. The Crossroad Publishing
Company, New York, 2000.

*Bernard of Clairvaux: A Lover Teaching the Way of
Love, Selected Spiritual Writings*. Introduced and
edited by M. Basil Pennington, O.C.S.O.
New City Press, New York, 1997.

*Love Without Measure: Extracts from the Writings of
Saint Bernard of Clairvaux*. Cistercian Studies
Series No. 127. Introduced and arranged by Paul
Diemer, OCSO. Cistercian Publications, 1990.

*St. Bernard of Clairvaux: Oracle of the Twelfth
Century*, by Theodore Ratisbonne. Tan Books and
Publishers, Inc, 1991.

Thomas Merton on Saint Bernard. Cistercian
Studies Series No. 9. Cistercian Publications,
1980.

The Wisdom Series:

Welcoming the New Millennium: Wisdom from Pope John Paul II

My Heart Speaks: Wisdom from Pope John XXIII

Live Jesus! Wisdom from Saints Francis de Sales and Jane de Chantal

A Radical Love: Wisdom from Dorothy Day

Walking with the Father: Wisdom from Brother Lawrence

Touching the Risen Christ: Wisdom from The Fathers

These popular books include short biographies of the authors and selections from their writings grouped around themes such as prayer, forgiveness, and mercy.

The New Testament Devotional Commentary Series:

Matthew: A Devotional Commentary

Mark: A Devotional Commentary

Luke: A Devotional Commentary

John: A Devotional Commentary

Acts of the Apostles: A Devotional Commentary

Leo Zanchettin, General Editor

Enjoy praying through the New Testament with commentaries that include each passage of scripture with a faith-filled meditation.

Books on Saints:

A Great Cloud of Witnesses: The Stories of 16 Saints and Christian Heroes by Leo Zanchettin and Patricia Mitchell

I Have Called You by Name: The Stories of 16 Saints and Christian Heroes by Patricia Mitchell

Each book contains inspiring biographies, along with selections of the saints' own writings.

**To order call 1-800-775-9673
or order online at www.wau.org**